From Wapping to Canary Wharf

The Journey of a Lifetime

David Exley

MADELEINE

ENJOY THE JOURNEY !

[signature]

Imprimata

Published by **Imprimata**

A CIP Catalogue record for this book is available
from the British Library

ISBN 978-1-906192-35-8

Set in Warnock Pro (InDCS4)

Printed in Great Britain

The poems reproduced in this book are credited
where authorship is known and appropriate
permissions have been obtained where possible.

Cover photograph © Siobhán Doran Photography
wwww.siobhandoran.com

Imprimata

Imprimata Publishers Limited
50 Albemarle Street, London W1S 4BD.

This book is dedicated to Mrs Kathleen Exley
The best Mum in the world !

Acknowledgements

Without the following people I could never have become the person I am today.

To Mum and Dad, thank you for creating me in the first place and for shaping my early years so well.

Dad, thank you for teaching me right from wrong and to have respect for my elders. I know I have also inherited your desire to entertain the people around me. Your premature death cheated me from knowing you as an adult and I missed not having that opportunity to grow with you.

Mum, thank you for showing me how important having a sense of humility is and how important it is just to be nice to absolutely everyone you come across. I see your influence every day in my own children's souls and I miss you as much now as I did the day I lost you over 30 years ago.

To my sister Pat, for taking on my Mother's role when we all needed an urgent replacement to keep us all together. To my brothers, sisters and their families for their understated love and affection.

To the management of Trollope & Colls who gave me the opportunity to achieve my first ambition, for allowing me to develop other skills and for putting up with me through the most truculent period of my working life.

To Harry Smith in particular. I never got to tell you how much I appreciated your efforts to keep me on the straight and narrow during my formative years at work.

To Vic Crespin for giving me the opportunity to move from the plant room to the office floor and for making management so much fun.

At Clifford Chance, to Keith Salway for your gentlemanly grace and charm and for giving a working class lad a chance at the big time, Keith Toms for teaching me to have patience, and Amanda Burton and Chris Turner for allowing me to have such an influence in London and around the world.

To my Wife's' parents, Henry and Eileen Kelly for all the emotional support and stability you have provided to Maria and me and my girls. To my daughters, Kelly and Louise, for being such an absolute credit to us and for being totally unaware of your own external and internal beauty.

To Maria for marrying me and blessing me with our two wonderful children. Maria, you have stood by me for over 26 years now, through good times and bad, even when things got so tough for me in the late '80s. I will never, ever forget that.

To Gian and Teresa Quattromini for being such good friends to Maria and me, and Jackie Preston for all the wonderful support provided to me at Clifford Chance over nearly 20 years.

Finally to one of my best friends Danny Ferry, who sadly passed away at Christmas 2008 and didn't live to see this book finished.

God bless you. This book is dedicated to you all.

David Exley
2009

Contents

Wapping circa 1950

Wapping is effectively an island, formed by the Thames on the left and the Dock Basins on the right.

These are (from top-bottom) St Katherines Dock, The Western Basin, The Eastern Basin and Shadwell Basin.

My Wapping birthplace, Riverside Mansions, can be seen to the left of the raised Garnet St road bridge in the centre of the photo.

To All Cockneys Leaving

To all cockneys leaving I'd just like to say
I'll miss you all dearly while you are away
I will always remember as it was before
Rows of old chimneys and old broken doors
Every door open and no need for keys
Your name was your token you were easy to please
Differences settled by clearing the air
Up with your fist was a strange old affair
Then off to the boozer and give me your hand
The best in the house, the best in the land
Then back to your chimneys and old broken doors
Sunday at my house and next week at yours.
Remember the era for it was your day
To all cockneys leaving I'd just like to say
I will miss you all dearly I'll wait your return
My door will be open and a coke fire will burn
To those who are leaving and for what you have been
Good bye you cockneys you're the cream of the cream

(Bruce Pope)

Preface

This poem says it all for me. Bruce Pope may have been describing any time at all over the last 150 years, but he sums up memories of the my place of birth, my home for 30 years and my emotions at moving from the area.

You can take the boy out of the East End but you can't take the East End of the boy.

This is the story of my life's journey from Wapping to Canary Wharf (1952-2009). These two places are geographically less than a mile apart in East London, but they are two very different worlds, and the changes in my life, and in this part of London over those 57 years have been incredible.

Wapping is an area of land in the London Docks formed by a small loop in the River Thames. Set on the North bank to the East of the Tower of London, it is bordered by The Highway, a main road to the north, and by the Thames itself to the South.

To visit or leave Wapping in my childhood, you'd need to cross one of many road bridges across the dock waterways. These bridges created a man-made island, defined Wapping as a place and a community, and almost certainly explain the extraordinary bonds that were formed amongst the people that I grew up with there.

For many years, the London Docks were the gateway to the world for Britain's imports and exports.

To many from outside the community, the docks were a dark, shadowy and dangerous place, full of thieves and vagabonds.

Sure, it was a tough, exciting place to live. We were also a community divided in two on religious grounds. You were either Catholic or Protestant and never the twain would meet. But it was my home and I wouldn't have wanted to grow up anywhere else.

Looking back over my life, most would say that the early

part was fairly tough and the latter part has been blessed.

I have become fairly successful in my adult life, but it hasn't always been plain sailing.

Shakespeare wrote in Twelfth Night "Some are born great, some achieve greatness and some have greatness thrust upon them".

I certainly wasn't born successful, far from it. Some of my success may have been thrust upon me. The rest came completely against the odds. I'm a working class East End boy, a "Wappingite", who did extremely well, nothing more and nothing less. I hope my life's story will act as a living example that anyone born on the wrong side of the tracks can still set seemingly impossible goals and achieve them.

I started life seven years after the 2nd World War ended, in a tough part of London's East End. I was born into a large and relatively poor family. My earliest ambition was to follow Dad's trade and use his union ticket to get work in the London Docks immediately outside my kitchen window. If I had done so, I could have become an unemployable ex-docker instead of now managing some of the most prestigious real estate in the world.

I left school at 15 in 1967. The London Docks were closing all around us. Instead of turning east and following the dock work as it moved downriver towards the Royal Docks and to Tilbury in Essex, I turned west and headed for the construction sites of the City of London.

Now aged 57 in 2009, I lead the Property Management team at the world's leading international law firm and manage one of the largest buildings on the Canary Wharf Estate in the heart of the revitalised London Docks area. A 1,027,278 sq ft, 35 storey building and I'm responsible for an annual £65 million budget spend that it takes just to occupy it.

I played a major part in the designs that created this award winning building and now have a team of over fifty staff who manage security, business continuity, fire protection, building insurance, cleaning, maintenance and health and safety. I'm also personally responsible for the property management, leases, rents, business rates, lettings, etc.

I travel the world to provide construction and design advice on office relocations. Between 2006/8, I registered 120,000 air miles with British Airways, travelling to, Delhi, Mumbai, Dubai, Abu Dhabi, New York, Washington, Moscow, Warsaw, Frankfurt, Prague, Dublin, Paris, Milan, Rome, Madrid, Luxembourg and Amsterdam.

I still cannot believe the changes in my circumstances and to the London Docks area I grew up in.

For years, I've just said I've been lucky, being in the right place at the right time. Some friends and colleagues tell me that I made my own luck along the way.

But I was in the wrong place on one cold night in the 1950s and lucky to have survived my childhood years at all. I'll tell you about that later.

When you read this book, I aim to make you laugh, shed a tear or two and hanker back to a better time. But I trust you will also be inspired by my story and take to heart the fact that, no matter how hard life gets, there's always the hope of better things to come.

David Exley, 2009

1952–1965
The Rock n Roll Years

*"Johnny slept with his head at the top of the bed with
Rob and me either side of him, with our heads by his
feet at the bottom of the bed"*

I was born on the 3rd of February 1952 in 218 Riverside Mansions, Garnet Street, Wapping, London, E1. Right in the heart of the London Docks, into a community divided in two, just as Northern Ireland had been, but without the levels of violence associated with that community.

I had an older brother, John, and an older sister, Pat. I was the second born of twin boys. Unlike me, Robert, my elder twin by 10 minutes, had been expected. I was such a surprise that I had no name initially and was called "the other one" for quite a while. People would visit and ask about Robert and then ask how "the other one" was.

One of my Aunties, it seems, insisted on calling me Ronald, but a visiting nurse called Nurse Knight eventually named me David.

Can you imagine it? Two sets of twins growing up in London's East End (a few years apart mind). Gangsters Ronnie and Reggie Kray in Bethnal Green and Ronnie and Robbie Exley living a mile or so away in Wapping. That could have been a recipe for disaster.

The family was completed two years after Rob and I were born when Catherine came along. She was the apple of my Dad's eye. He always called her "Princess".

My mum was actually born in Liverpool and not in London. She had an older brother, Harry, an older sister, Eileen, and a younger brother and sister, Wilf and Rose. Her own mum had died giving birth to my Aunt Rosie

Henry Blakeney (Mum's Dad) was born in Margate, Kent, and had moved to Liverpool. A few years after Mum's own mother had died; he met and married the lady I only ever knew to be my Nan. She was Martha Panracker. "Nanny Blake" to me.

Shortly after Henry married Martha, he suddenly died! So Nanny Blake then had five school kids to bring up and none them her own. They don't make women like this anymore, do they?

Nanny Blake was the Matriarch of the family at the time I was born.

My mum was one of 5 kids who had lost both parents at a very young age. My dad, too, was one of 5 kids. He had two sisters, Betty and Margie, and two brothers, Danny and Robert (Monty).

Unlike my older brother John, who can remember my dad's mother, Julia Exley, I never knew any of my four real grandparents at all. Just Nanny Blake.

She lived in an identical mansion block to Riverside Mansions called Regents House. It was in Limehouse. It's gone now. But we'd visit her regularly as kids and, as soon as we came through the door, she would drag us to the sink and wash our faces, necks and hands before we got any tea from her. We must have been a scruffy load of scamps.

I remember thinking it was a good idea to take my little sister Catherine and myself up to see her one day. I might have been about eight years old and Catherine just six. I suppose I should have told someone first!

Nanny Blake was not happy to see us that day at all. In fact, she went mad at me. She lived about three quarters of a mile from our home and I had to cross two major roads, The Highway and the Commercial Road, to get there.

I also took Catherine up to Earl's Court Olympia to see the Boys and Girls Exhibition once. Again we were far too young to be out on own. Keith Fordyce, the compere of the pop show "Ready, Steady, Go!", was one of the celebrities at the show. I lost her there and the police brought me home separately. Thank God Catherine reported herself to the security guards in the hall. I didn't do it again.

Nanny Blake had a big aspidistra and some ostrich feathers in a vase and loads of Victorian furniture. I can also remember some framed fabrics depicting Chinese scenes. The landing of the dwellings looked out on to Regents Canal, which fed into Limehouse docks, and there was a big factory chimney with "Lusty's Turtle Soup" written on it, which always amused me whenever I saw it. I couldn't imagine ever eat eating a soup with a turtle swimming around in it.

Nanny Blake died in 1962.

Our life was not all doom and gloom though.

My dad, John Exley, a former Army regular prior to the 2nd World War, was now a London docker; my mum, Kathleen, had worked in a cigarette factory during the war and was now a cleaner, part-time barmaid and shop assistant.

218 Riverside Mansions was a two bedroomed flat on level 2 of an old

mansion block of dwellings. There were seven of us living here.

Unlike the tower blocks built in the 1970s with just four flats on each lift landing, Riverside was formed by three rows of maisonettes, a ground floor row with gardens front and rear and two upper levels of maisonettes connected by long open balconies that ran the whole length of the premises, forming continuous terraces of 100 flats on each level.

This may explain how they created a happy community within them. They were "ground-scrapers". We called them flats because maisonettes sounded too posh for us.

There was a lift in the middle of the estate for upper floor tenants who had to use a Yale key to call it to a landing and use it again to choose a floor to travel to, once inside. The lift was never vandalised as kids were not given a key, and we didn't vandalise things anyway back then.

The blocks were arranged to form an extended "E" and they had three large open squares in them, where we played as children.

There was a genuine community spirit in Riverside, and every family in the 300 flats all knew each other well.

There were times when I'd see some more modern single building homes and would wonder what it would be like to live in them. They were called "prefabs". I thought that was because they were so "fabulous". But it turned out these were the prefabricated, asbestos clad, temporary homes that were erected to replace the housing stock that was lost in the blitz.

I know the people who lived in them liked them very much. They were probably a step up in quality from some of the slums they used to live in. But they were "temporary" for far too long for most people.

We 5 kids all slept in the one bedroom in Riverside and Mum and Dad were in the other one.

The sleeping arrangements? Well, Mum and Dad had their own bed, of course, in the bedroom overlooking the open square where we played. Pat and Catherine slept in one double bed, while Robert and John and I slept another, in the other bedroom overlooking the Docks. Johnny slept with his head at the top of the bed, with Rob and me either side of him, with our heads by his feet at the bottom of the bed. I later used to joke that I'd have liked to sleep in the shallow end one night! But we were a close-knit, supportive family unit and we didn't wet the bed…that much.

Seems a bit cramped? It was, but we didn't know any better.

We also had a dog, a cat, a budgie and, at times, pet mice and rats, and I even had some terrapins in the bathtub until Mum saw them. Our first dog was a little white mongrel called Butch. He turned out to be a she and had five pups in an upturned tea chest in the kitchen. Pat and John stayed up all night with her. We kept one of the pups, a little black female called Suzie. Dad called our cat Tommy-Tiddle-Mouse, and the budgie (in fact any budgie we had over those early years) was called Joe-Budge.

Mum and Dad didn't have money to throw around but we'd have a few treats to look forward to each week, if we'd been good.

Thursday night was comic night. Everyone would get one and we'd swap them with each other. There was The Dandy, The Beano, The Topper, The Victor, and Bunty for the girls. I used to love reading about the toffs in these comics. It was like another world to me. The Victor also had many war hero stories, and I used to imagine my Dad being just like them: killing Nazis single-handedly and never mentioning it.

Some Fridays all the kids would gang up on Mum and Dad and chant aloud together: "We always have a nosh on a Friday... We always have a nosh on a Friday..." Mum would always give in and one of us would be sent over to the off licence in the Jolly Sailor pub for packets of crisps, a bottle of lemonade or cream soda and maybe a bar of fruit and nut. Crisps in those days came in just the one flavour, potato flavour, and there was a little blue paper wrap inside that had salt in it.

Then we would all settle down for a night in front of the telly. There might have been something scary on like Quattermass, and we'd hide behind the sofa, or maybe something funny like the Army Game, I Love Lucy, Bilko, or Bootsie and Snudge. Peyton Place, the American soap series, was a favourite too.

We were silly but happy!

Rob and I were identical twins in the medical sense but we weren't so identical. He was never really that keen on being a twin and always wanted to dress and even act differently. We grew up with different mates at school too.

Using a 60s analogy, I was a Beatle and he was a Rolling Stone. That sums us up, really.

He was a shy kid and I was always more outgoing, and that didn't change much throughout our lives. Maybe his shyness was due to a terrible stutter he was cursed with as a kid.

We kids weren't really aware that we were poor, as we were surrounded by families far worse off than us and we didn't travel much further than Wapping in those days, so we could not compare our living standards with those of other families.

Our home was freezing in winter. The windows weren't double-glazed, as most are these days, and the wind would whistle through the gaps around them and the external doors. There was a coal fire downstairs in the living room, and, just before we went to bed, we would open the doors from the front room to the bedrooms to let some heat up into them. I used to jiggle around in bed to create some friction in the bedclothes to generate some heat to get myself warm in the winter months.

Once a fortnight or so we'd get a coal delivery from Charlie Ryder, the local coalman. Can you imagine this now? He'd walk straight in crunching coal into the corridor lino and shoot a hundredweight of coal straight into the cupboard under the stairs, shake the sack out and walk out again. The flat would be liberally dusted with coal dust for a day or so.

The ashes from the previous night's fire would have to be cleared from the fireplace every day and the new fire prepared and lit. A broadsheet newspaper would be held across the front of the fireplace to create a draught through the fire that was made up from screwed up paper and sticks of wood. Once that got going, you could add the coal. It was quite a task, and you were only allowed to do it once you had been educated by Mum or Dad, or by one of the older kids.

Many is the time that one of us would be running through the house with the newspaper on fire or shouting "Mum the paper's gone up the chimney! What do we do now?"

I always used to marvel at how Father Christmas got down that little fireplace every year. But that was the magic of Christmas.

There was a flat roof on top of Riverside Mansions, so it all made sense at the time.

We had a stove in the kitchen into which we put coal too. It had a hot plate on the top, so you could put a kettle on it. We used to love crowding round that to get warm in the winter, after running round the balconies in the snow.

I don't remember ever having a pair of wellingtons, but I do remember the chilblains we got from having freezing cold feet in winter. We tended to have a pair of shoes for best and a pair of "rubbers" for school and for playing out in. Posher people called them plimsolls. Mine always seem to wear out early and I'd cut up packets of discarded cereal boxes into the shapes of soles and insert them into my rubbers whenever I had holes in the soles. I didn't want to get into trouble for wearing them out too quickly.

This did not work, of course, in the winter or the rainy months, but you could get another month out of them in the summer.

There were no private houses in Wapping, apart from the big Georgian ones where the nun's convent was, or the old Dock Master's house at Pier head. They are worth a fortune now, but they formed the local medical centre then. We used to go there and be inoculated against measles and chicken pox and get our hair combed by posh old nurses who searched us for head lice. We used to call them the "Nitty Noras". I never had any nits as Dad always insisted us boys had an army style "short back and sides" haircut.

Dad would send Robert and me up to Sid and Maurice's barbers shop on Commercial Road. They were a nice couple of old boys.

Rob and I were so small we had to sit on a board that the barbers put across the arms of the chair. We hated getting our hair cut, though, as the old boys used to sing to us while we were in the chair. There were a couple of popular children's serials on TV at the time, "Davy Crockett" and "Robin Hood".

So, when it was my turn, I'd have to put up with a very Jewish version of Davy Crockett.

"Davey... Davey Crockett...King of da vild frontier", etc. Then Rob would have to endure:

"Robin Hood ...Robin Hood riding through da glen.

Robin Hood... Robin Hood viv 'is band a men,

Feared by da bad,

Loved by da good,

Robin Hood...Robin Hood"

We were mortified every single time.

Sid and his colleagues were still cutting my hair into my 30s at his unisex salon, "The International", in Whitechapel, in the 1980s. So I must have forgiven him.

Dockers' families in the 50s and 60s couldn't afford to own property, and never wanted to, come to that. We used to say, "Why would you want to own a place when it's cheaper to live in a council flat, and the council come round and decorate it every 4 years for free, too." The use of casual labour in the docks created a variable flow of income in any case.

Registered dockers who had permanent employment and casuals, who got work as when it was available, divided the dock labour force.

Can you imagine anyone today queuing up twice each day to get work, as the casual labour dockers had to? The foreman would come out and select a few big and strong looking dockers and perhaps a few of his own mates, and then toss the remaining job tokens in the air and let the remaining dockers fight over them.

When the docks were nationalised, things got a bit better. If a causal labour docker did not get any work, he could go and "Bomp on" to get the minimum wage from the National Dock Labour Board. It's no wonder there were so many strikes, etc. I used to see the lads, meeting on the bombsites, listening to Jack Dash, the communist union leader.

It seems quite odd to me that they will now be remembered as being greedy, or holding the country to ransom, when they only trying to protect their livelihood and put some food on the table for their families.

They weren't killed off by their union activities. Their jobs went because the London Docks were built for smaller ships and not for the huge vessels you see today. But it was containerisation that really done for them. These guys were used to pulling sacks of coffee and stuff about with hooks. My Dad's docker's hook hung in the larder in 6 Riverside Mansions for many years after he died, and I wish I'd kept hold of it, now, as a keepsake, to help describe to my kids the hard tasks that he had to do.

After containerisation revolutionised the handling of ships' cargo, these guys were no longer needed in anything like the numbers in the 50s, and, where they were needed was downriver, where the new container docks were being built. But you needed very few dockers there, too.

The local homes reflected the nature of the work and the pay. They were very small and of low quality, and mainly council owned.

There were some private slum dwellings in Wapping, like those in Prusom St and Watts St Mansions and Old Tower Buildings. They had no bathrooms, central heating or lifts, and they were far from being mansions.

The maisonettes in Riverside Mansions had no central heating either. Those on the ground floor had an outside toilet with no form of heat or light. The bath was in small room off the kitchen. But hot water was supplied by the landlord's boilers to the kitchen sink and the bath from a central boiler house. The locals still considered it the best place to live in Wapping, even though we had to wash our face and hands each day in the kitchen sink.

We did have an electric cooker point with a 15 amp round pin socket on it, and there was a 5-amp socket at the bottom of the stairs for a fridge. There was another 15-amp socket and another 5-amp outlet in the front room and one more outlet in the larger of the two bedrooms. But that was it.

Mum and Dad bought an electric two-bar fire with fake coals, lit by a red 40w bulb, but it would invariably blow a fuse unless we unplugged something else first. But using that fire really ate into the household funds. So it was not used much, and we always kept the living room door closed to keep the heat in.

This was a time when every home had a coin operated electricity meter. So, every other day, we'd be plunged into darkness and had to pop next door to borrow a shilling for the meter, light a candle, then stand on a chair to feed the shilling in and turn the lever to start the meter going again. That was followed by a big cheer when the telly, cooker and lights came back on again. A chap from the electricity board would come round once a month and take the coins away. Some people would break into the meter and keep feeding the same shilling in over and over again. They were in trouble when he came round, and he'd cut them off if they did not pay up what they owed.

Our clothes iron used to be plugged into the light bulb outlet in the ceiling via an adaptor, which was handy as you could iron clothes in the centre of the room.

If we had any music of our own it would come from large breakable 78-rpm records, the size of dinner plates.

We'd listen to stars such as Winifred Attwell playing her piano, Ruby Murray singing "Softly, Softly", Shirley Bassey singing "As long as he needs me", Alma Cogan singing "Never do a tango with an Eskimo" or "Sugar in the morning, sugar in the evening, sugar at supper-time", The Beverley Sisters singing "Sisters, Sisters, there were never such devoted sisters", Lonnie Donegan, Elvis Presley, The Everley Brothers. The first 78rpm recording we ever had was "The Laughing Policemen".

These were very different times to those of today. We had a small black and white TV, but the picture was never great. I loved the telly and we'd never miss children's favourite "Watch with Mother" and "Mr Pastry "in the daytime. "Rag, Tag and Bobtail" was another favourite, too.

In the evening, we'd come home from school to watch "Pancho and Cisco", a pair of crime-fighting Mexican cowboys. Dad would always take the mickey out of the programme and say. "You watch, any minute now Pancho will climb up on the roof of that ranch house and he'll jump down on the baddies as they come out". He was right too, they always did. How did he know?

The programme always finished with Pancho lamenting "Oh, Cisco!" and The Cisco Kid always said "Oh, Pancho" back.

We'd also watch The Lone Ranger and Tonto, Gene Autrey and

Champion, the Wonder Horse.

I'd put my guns, cowboy hat and sheriff's badge on and sit across the arms of our settee to pretend to be riding a horse, and capture all the Indians. We had guns that fired blanks in those days. Cap guns they were called. You'd feed a paper tape reel into the revolver, and it had little gunpowder discs on it that gave a real crack and produced a puff of smoke when you fired your guns.

This was a time when there were just two TV channels to chose from, BBC or ITV. Nothing else and no remote control units either. We kids were our parent's remote control. "Turn it over for me," they'd say, and we'd get out of the chair and do it.

The TV programmes always ended before midnight then, but not until the National Anthem was played each night. When you turned the telly off, the screen went dead but for a little white dot left in the middle of the screen and it got smaller and smaller until, five minutes later, it was gone. We kids used to peer into it to see what was going on behind the scenes. Were they packing things up in the studio maybe?

We also had a second-hand "reel to reel" tape recorder but it was never much cop.

Radio was still big in those days. We had a gramophone, a walnut cabinet with a huge radio dial on the front. You could hear all kinds of foreign languages as you turned the dial. But you'd search for the Light Service or the Home Service to get something you could understand.

After the gramophone finally broke down, our Uncle Wilf, who had been in the RAF and was into radio engineering, made us a record player out of a tea chest. I remember it had a thick stylus like a drawing pin.

We had no video recorders, CD players or any of the paraphernalia we all must have now. They weren't invented then, of course, and, if they had been, we certainly couldn't have afforded them.

The wealthy may have had a telephone in their homes, but it was beyond the means of Wappingites in the 50s and, let's face it, we had nobody we could phone up anyway.

Policeman still walked the streets on the beat and the only form of communication they had was a whistle.

Night watchmen still sat around coke braziers at night to look after any road works. Their job was to keep the red Tilley lamps that hung from the wooden barriers around excavations, topped up with paraffin oil all night. We'd sit with them and they'd tell us kids scary stories.

This was a time when kids had to been seen and not heard.

The key to our home hung from a piece of string behind the letterbox. When you came home, you put your hand through the letterbox and pulled the string through and opened the door with the key. Everyone did the same in the East End, and everyone knew where all the front door keys were hanging. But no one broke into your homes. Mind you, we had bugger all worth nicking if anyone did.

We did not have washing machines. Mum did that by hand and used a "mangle" to squeeze the water out of the washing. This was a contraption set up in the bathroom, consisting of wooden rollers through which you passed your clean, wet washing. As you turned its huge handle the rollers squeezed the water out into a carefully placed bucket below it. I used to like to see how far a bed sheet would go through before it folded over into the bath.

We didn't have supermarkets. Harry Stewart was our local grocer and he ran the tiny shop on the corner of Riverside Mansions with his wife May. They lived in what I thought was the posher part of Riverside. He was a proper grocer and sliced cold meat as thick or as thin as you wanted it. If you asked for a tin of beans he would knock them down from the top shelf some 15 ft from the floor with a long pole with a hook on it and catch them every time. I never saw him drop one in 30 years.

We used to have "a tab" in there, because we did not always have enough money to pay. He'd remind us next time we came in though and we had to pay up before we could have any more on the tab. If we were still too skint to pay him off we would shop in Wapping Lane instead.

You could judge the commercial climate of the whole country by how many, and how long, the tabs were in his shop.

If the economy was doing badly, there was a clear correlation between that, International Trade and the docker's wages.

We also used to collect the stamps from the packets of Horniman's tea. You'd fill a book with them and collect your divvy (dividend) when you brought it back to the shop. Perhaps a free packet of tea.

We used to love visiting our Aunties and Uncles in Dagenham in Essex. It was about 8 miles from Wapping and totally different to the Docks area. The homes there were council houses, not flats, and there were trees just growing in places. No one had even planted them there on purpose!

We'd always have salads at Auntie Rosie's (Mum's sister) and we never did eat that stuff in Wapping, really. Fruit, yes, but not salads. We were more your Egg and Chips brigade. Even now I can't eat cucumber without the taste immediately transporting me back to the '50s and Sunday afternoon teas in Dagenham. Rosie and Eddie had moved there from the council flats called Matilda House up near the Tower of London. Eddie worked at the Ford car plant.

We didn't see so much of Dad's side, who also lived also in Dagenham. I think they were at bit stuck up.

We loved our fish and chips, too, and I can still recall coming back to Riverside from Wapping Lane in the winter all warm and cosy with 5 or 6 portions of fish and chips on my chest. Chips just don't seem as hot as they were then. Or, perhaps, I don't want to smell of fish now and don't clutch them so close to me anymore. We'd always ask the shop owner for some crackling, too. This was just lumps of batter that were floating around in the fryer. It was free and would have been thrown away, anyway.

Pie and mash in Watney St came high on our list of treats, too, and I'd always have "two and two, please" on a Saturday lunchtime. That's two meat pies and two spoonfuls of mash, with a dollop of green parsley liquor all over it. We'd then pour on loads of salt and pepper and vinegar and wolf it down with a spoon and fork; never, ever, did we use a knife, licking the plate when you'd finished, too

Prior to that, we'd have been to Saturday morning "pictures" at the Troxy, or to the "Penny Bughole" in Commercial Road, where we'd watch a cartoon, a feature film and a serial.

Again, there was a song to go with it, and the whole audience would sing it as "Uncle Charlie", or whatever his name was, rose out of the orchestra pit playing a large concert organ.

"We come along on Saturday mornings
Greeting everybody with a smile
We come along on Saturday mornings..."

Uncle Charlie always got pelted with ice cream packets as he desperately tried to get away under the stage, having descended, under fire, when he'd finished his bit.

I used to love watching Norman Wisdom at the pictures; he was hilarious. He always played the little guy that did well and got the girl in the end.

Whenever we went to the Troxy, we had to walk past the Barnado's children's home. It had two large brass push plates on the front doors that were engraved to simulate two big open doors.

We used to speed up as we went past in case the people who ran the place grabbed us and pulled us in. Not that they would, but we didn't know that at the time. Great memories.

There were times when we'd go to the "new park" on the river in Shadwell to paddle in the pool and have jam sandwiches as a treat. Sometimes we'd watch a film on the mobile cinema that would tour the parks. It was a big lorry/coach thing with a large screen and loudspeakers on it.

Street vendors were another feature of 1950s Wapping.

We'd eat fried kippers with malt vinegar on them on Saturday nights and we always looked forward to a seafood supper on Sunday evenings. Cockles, whelks, pickled herrings and some winkles maybe. My sister Pat had the patience of a saint and would spend hours picking hundreds of winkles from their shells to make just one winkle sandwich. We'd all collect the hard caps that were removed from the winkles' heads and we'd put them on our faces and say they were beauty spots.

We'd buy the seafood from a scruffy old bloke who came around the streets on a horse and cart. His name was Dan, and he kept his horses in a derelict fire station in Shadwell.

We'd all sing a song about him.

"Dan, Dan, the winkle man,

Sold 'is fish from a watering can,

Washed 'is face in a frying pan,

Dan, Dan, the winkle man".

We also used to look forward to the Toffee Apple Man's arrival. He'd enter the square of Riverside Mansions on his bike and call out "Toffee Apples!" and toot his horn, "Parp, Parp!"

We'd all call out to our Mums for a few coins to buy them from him. Great big apples on a stick, with hard crunchy syrup covering them. The Mums would wrap the coins in a piece of paper and throw them down from the balconies so the coins would not roll all over the square and get lost.

There were still the Rag and Bone men in the streets on their horse and carts. You'd give them your old clothes in exchange for a plastic Addis washing up bowl or a few coins. Recycling or what?

There was also an old boy with a limp and an arm missing who used to beg for money. He had a flat cap and a big drooping moustache like a brush. He wore an old raincoat down to his ankles upon which he wore a long row of medals and a sign saying "Disabled War Veteran". I'm not sure that he was a war veteran, or even disabled, come to that. But he'd sing some miserable dirge that no one could understand, and people would feel sorry for him and give him a few coins to bugger off. I never believed he had lost an arm at all.

This was a time when horses were still pulling goods around the streets, so there were still horse's troughs on the pavements at major road junctions. These were full of fresh water, and, above them, hung big brass cups on chains so you could get a cold drink in the street, yourself, from the taps that filled the troughs.

The horses would then be fed by the draymen who would hang a straw bag full of oats, etc., over the horse's heads, and the old nags would stand and eat from them, shaking the bags violently to get the last oat from them. I still say to this day that I am going out to get some "nosebag" when I tell my work colleagues I'm off out to lunch.

On some Sundays, a trotting cart would also come down to Wapping and you could have a ride around the local streets for 3d, the equivalent of just over 1p in today's money. The cart would take maybe four people in the back plus two more sitting at the front with the driver. We'd let it get moving then hang onto the back for a free ride where the driver could not see us. It was dangerous as you could fall off into the path of a car, but there weren't too many cars on the roads at that time.

My Dad would leap from his chair in those years whenever he heard a horse and cart go by. He'd grab the coal shovel from the fireplace and come back with some fresh horse manure for his roses in the garden. Sometimes another docker would beat him to it, though.

I don't remember using a tram as my older brother John can, but I do remember trolley buses. These were just like the traditional London buses we see today but they were electrical rather than petrol-engine powered. They had long poles above their roofs that connected to overhead electrical wires that ran the lengths of the streets. We'd stand and watch as the bus driver changed them over from one track to another, at Leman Street, so they could then make a return journey. Sparks would fly as they did it, and we were always amazed at how they avoided getting an electric shock in the process.

Some Saturdays, we'd walk up to the Tower of London. There used to be a Scotsman and his mate who entertained the tourists on a big cobbled square. He'd crack an enormous whip over his head to get the crowd's attention and then put his mate into a sack, padlock chains around him and place swords through the chains. His mate had to get out of the sack in four minutes or he'd suffocate, apparently. He always got out, but we'd always come back every other week to see if he would die or not.

Sometimes we'd go down onto the beach on the riverfront, in front of traitor's gate at the Tower of London. It sounds absolutely crazy now, but there was a sandy beach installed there, and there was a deckchair attendant too. Honest.

If we got bored, we'd dodge the ticket office at Wapping, get on the underground and go up to Paddington or Kings Cross stations and watch the steam trains coming and going. That was great fun and these big stations were very exciting places to be. The air was full of the smell of the smoke from the engines and the sound of the trains' steam whistles and the slamming of carriage doors.

Sunday dinners were always looked forward to. Mum excelled at cooking these and we'd have roast beef and huge Yorkshire puddings with roast potatoes and "greens" in those days. This I later learned to be cabbages and cauliflowers, of course. But we called all vegetables our "greens".

I'd always clean up my whole dinner. Dad used to call me "Billy Bangers", after all the sausages I'd put away. I used to make a scene at Christmas when the legs and wings from the turkey were being divvied out. I used to claim the "Parson's Nose" every year, as there was only one of them. I didn't know what it was then, of course, and quickly dropped eating them in my teenage years when I found out.

We'd watch Liberace on the telly on Sunday afternoons or an old black and white film with Fred Astaire and Ginger Rodgers, or, maybe, the Marks Brothers, in it. The music of the day was heavily influenced by US stars like Nat King Cole and Sammy Davis Junior who were black men trying to be white and, of course, Dad's favourites, the Black and White Minstrels, who were white men blacked up to look like black men. How odd is that?

I loved my food and always scoffed down my school meals too. Chocolate Pudding and Chocolate Custard was my favourite. In fact, I used to eat everything and anything that came my way and still do.

We were poor enough to be granted free school meals while others in my class had to pay. That should have been a clue to our poverty status, but, basically, I thought more fool you if you paid for it.

Patty Commons was the girl in our class who used to be the dinner money monitor and she would collect the Shilling from those who paid. She would just shake the tin when the kids on free school meals approached her in the line, simulating the coin dropping in to avoid embarrassing them.

It was at junior school that I first fell in love. It was a case of love at first sight and I was besotted with her. Her name was Kathleen and she was stunning. She was tall and had long brown hair tied in a ponytail. She had lovely skin too. A sort olive shade and she could have passed for an Italian. Looking back, she looked like a 1960's Pocahontas.

I'd carry her books home every night from Wapping to Cuttle Close in Shadwell. Even though David Norbury would be waiting for me at the bridge in Wapping Lane. He was an ogre and wanted to beat the shit out of me every night. I always got past him ok and would still walk her home, even if he did catch me. Kathleen could sing and dance, too, and I spend the whole of our Irish Dancing lessons trying to get myself positioned opposite her, so that, when we had to dance in pairs, I'd get to hold her hand. Real puppy love stuff, eh? The purist of love; no sex involved at all.

Shame she was the fastest runner in the school after Alan Lawler. Whenever we played Kiss Chase with the girls in Wapping Park, I could never catch her!

As a family, we all helped support ourselves, and the boys would have newspaper rounds, picking the daily papers from Dooley's paper shop in Commercial road and delivering them all over Stepney. It brought in a few quid.

Rob and I also used to work for a bloke named Gerry in Shadwell. We used to deliver paraffin oil in one-gallon cans to the slum buildings in the area. We use to fill his steel cans from the back of the tanker via a funnel, then carry them, four at a time, up the old dwelling buildings and into the homes of the elderly. Some people were lonely and bed-ridden, so we'd fill the paraffin heaters for them and they'd give us a little tip.

We stank of paraffin and I'm sure we would have gone up in smoke if we had come close to anyone with a lit cigarette. Everyone remembers where he or she was in 1963 when they heard that US President John F. Kennedy had been shot dead in Dallas Texas. I was 11 years old and pouring paraffin into cans outside Riverside Mansions at the time.

Mum's Brother, Uncle Wilf, and his wife, Aunt Vi, were great fun and a real "win double" in those days. They had a daughter, my cousin, Irene. They lived in Limehouse, close to Nanny Blake, in one of those "walk up" three storey flats that populated the area.

They always reminded me of Stan and Hilda Ogden or Jack and Vera Duckworth from Coronation Street: always pulling each other's legs and slagging each other off. But we used to wet ourselves at the two them.

Vi's parents, Mr and Mrs Wren, were still alive and well in the 1960s and lived in Raines Mansions in Wapping (which were no mansions, I can tell you).

Old Billy Wren still wore those black baggy trousers, open waistcoat;

collar-less white shirt, and brown belt and braces that men in the 1930s would wear.

Wapping was a man-made island. We had the Thames surrounding us on one side and the dock basins on the other, and everyone had to cross one of many bridges to get to or from it.

These bridges, ships, barges, lorries, horse and carts, high walls and cranes dominated our lives. Try telling your schoolteachers in Bethnal Green that you were late for school because "I caught a bridger, Sir" and they would look at you as if you came from another planet. To tell the truth we all thought we were different, coming from Wapping. It's that Islander mentality; to us, if you weren't from the Dock's community, you weren't worth knowing, anyway.

"Catching a bridger", by the way, is what happens when a ship comes into the docks from the Thames and it has to pass through the various dock basins and lock gates that controlled the height of the water in them. The Thames is tidal, don't forget. The road bridges would roll back, and the section that crossed the waterways would stand as high as three or four double-decker buses while the ships passed through.

So, when you heard the bridge bells ringing, you had to run like mad to get over the bridge before they closed the road to traffic and pedestrians and raised it for the ships.

As kids, we used to attend Wapping Youth Club, which was held in the disused Fire Station in Watts St. But the docks, the warehouses and even the river were our favourite playground. Container ships and lorries weren't invented then, so the streets were full of canvas-covered lorries of all shapes and sizes. They were filthy, but great fun to play on. Dad would come and get us if we stayed out too late, and would kick our arses all the way home. He could still manage it with his painful limp! We'd then get a good "scruffing" when we got home. Dad would give us a real rough wash over the kitchen sink and, if it hurt you, or he got soap got in your eyes, tough! We'd then get a good walloping and be sent to bed crying. That happened often when we were kids. Tough love.

The River Police came into our school once a year and would us tell us all off and show how dangerous the river was in particular. We did lose one of our schoolmates, Bernard May, to the river. He must have been about eight years old when he drowned under a barge, poor sod. His Mum never, ever got over it.

I still miss now the sound of the ships blasting their horns. They'd do it all together at midnight on New Year's Eve. We'd all run to the windows and open them up to hear them bringing in the New Year.

We were surrounded by bombsites and what we called "debrees" (debris). These were the wrecked buildings from the 2nd World War Blitz of London, and we would set up campsites on the open land or play Cowboys and Indians in the war damaged buildings.

They were the 1950s equivalent of the adventure playgrounds of today. Unsupervised and more dangerous, of course, but, I tell you, they were more fun than any health and safety approved playground of today. We'd play on the "Rubber Dump" in Solander Gardens, which was a mountain of rubber gas masks and army surplus rubber tyres and stuff. Jumping off the very high walls that surrounded it onto this stuff was great fun. There was the old Jam Factory at the top of Wapping Lane. We'd hide in its huge ovens and pretend to be Jews getting gas in the gas chambers!

We'd also pop into the docker's cafe that my Mum managed for a couple of better-off East Enders. It was painted bright red and the address was 210 The Highway. It was opposite the "Rubber Dump". One of the owners, Harold Lee, drove a great big petrol tanker, and I used to go out in it with him delivering fuel to petrol stations and depots all over the South East of England.

I can remember how he "cleaned me" (told me off) once when I jumped down from the cab on the passenger's side, as I always did. But, on this particular occasion, I'd jumped down into the traffic. I was really upset at the time, but I now know he was only so upset because he cared for me. I've never forgotten that telling off. Perhaps it was because it did not include the belting that Dad would have given me.

Wapping - a divided community

*"We'd stop the procession for a few minutes outside
the Protestant church and Tommy Leek, a huge
Docker, who always played our huge bass drum held
high on his huge chest, would bang it just a bit louder
before we moved off again"*

We were not particularly religious but we were brought up in the Catholic faith. There were two schools in Wapping, St Patrick's, the Roman Catholic school, or St Peters, the Church of England school. To get into and stay at St Pats, you had to go to church every Sunday.

This may seem odd today but there was a huge divide between the two religions in Wapping and you could just as easily have been in Northern Ireland in the 1950's and early 1960's. We weren't killing each other. But we did not mix or even talk to the Protestants, really. We were all cockneys with Irish names.

Each year, the Catholics and the Protestants would have their respective marching processions, with banners, statues, flutes, drums and bagpipes. We'd stop the procession for a few minutes outside the Protestant church and Tommy Leek, a huge Docker, who always played our huge bass drum held high on his huge chest, would bang it just a bit louder before we moved off again.

The marches were held in May when we would crown our Queen of the May and the youngest kids in the junior school would have their first communion. I was usually a banner holder, a position high in the procession pecking order. After that would be a reserve banner holder who would take over if it got too windy.

One year, it was Henry Ferris, and I wouldn't let him have a turn of holding the banner. I kept telling him "My Mum has not taken my photo with her Box Brownie camera yet", just so I could hold it proudly the whole way round the procession.

Down the pecking order from that came the kids who held one of the strings attached to a banner. Then came the dross that just walked at the edge of the parade. We called them "the gutter walkers". They would get covered in muck and rainwater from the gutters at the side of the road if it had recently rained.

This was always a great time for Wapping. Any Wappingites who had moved away would come back to Wapping for that weekend. They would follow the band into Wapping and follow them back to Tower Hill, or wherever. At the end of the evening, the band would lead the Parish Priest around the streets and he would bless all the altars that would be put out in the gardens. We had great songs like "Our Glorious Saint Patrick" and "God Bless Our Pope" and "Ave Maria". Irish rebel songs would be sung in the pubs and social clubs once the adults had a few drinks in them. But we stopped singing them in 1969 when the troubles kicked off in Northern Ireland again.

This must all sound very odd now, but we were the descendants of Irish immigrants. There's even a Wapping Docks in Liverpool.

We had some lovely schoolteachers, and some right bastards, too. Sisters of Mercy, who wore huge winged headdresses and veils and long black robes, ran the local schools. Sister Mary, the headmistress of the junior school, would show you no mercy at all, and kept the cane tucked away inside her robe.

Sister Teresa was a kindly old soul though. She was the head of the infant school. We had a lovely teacher there called Miss Whitmore. She called us all her "Honey bunches", and she had a chatterbox table where she would put all the kids that talked too much. Katherine Cooper and I were permanent residents on it.

Miss Hanley, who was much older than the other teachers, was a very tough but very fair teacher. She had the class of kids that had just left the nursery. I can still recall going to sleep on a canvas camp bed, pillow and blanket in the nursery school playground in the afternoons. I absconded once and climbed over the school wall and ran home to Mum because they were making me eat lettuce in vinegar. Yuck!

Miss Casey in the junior school was another tough cookie but someone who loved us too. She played the violin to us in singing lessons and would stamp her feet when she got mad.

To confirm that we had actually been at church on the previous Sunday the teachers would ask us randomly what colour vestments the priest had worn at mass. If you'd missed mass, you'd guess and sometimes you'd get it right. It was usually green or yellow. If you then got it wrong you were in double trouble for lying as well as missing church.

On Sunday afternoons, the priest would knock on all the Catholics' doors to collect money for the church. Dad would leave half a crown on the arm of the settee he was sitting in and pretend to be asleep, so that he didn't have to talk to him. The priest would pick it up, pocket it and bless us all.

Following your baptism as a baby and your first communion in junior school, the next stage in a Catholic's life is your confirmation. This is where you chose to stay with the church of your own volition (yeah, right!). You get to choose your own confirmation name, too. Most of the girls would choose Mary, Teresa or Bernadette and the boys would go for Matthew, Mark, Luke, John or Peter after various Saints and Apostles.

Well, sod that for a game of soldiers. I chose Tarcicius! He was a brave young boy who delivered communion wafers to persecuted Catholics who celebrated mass in underground caves in Rome. He was mugged for them one day and when the crooks searched him the communion wafers had disappeared. It was a miracle! This would be my secret name I thought. But it did not stay a secret for long.

We all had to line up in front of the Bishop, kiss the foot of the cross and then his ring and tell him what our confirmation name was so he could bless us with it. All was going well until I got to him.

"And your name will be?" asks the Bishop. "Tarcicius", I say proudly. "Pardon", he says. "Tarcicius", I repeat, a little louder this time. "Oh. Right...", he says. I then look over my shoulder and there's Michael Murphy one of the biggest jokers in the school with his hand over his mouth, laughing his head off. He couldn't wait to tell everyone.

Shit. My secret was out. Michael still teases me mercilessly about it to this very day. Now you all know my secret, too.

Anyone for run outs?

"Ally, ally in. We're not playing, Cat's got the measles!"
...What was that all about?

We'd moved from number 218, on the top balcony in Riverside, down to number 6 when I was about 11, in 1963. This was great because we now had a small garden at the back and to front of the maisonette. Charlie Packenham formerly occupied it; he was one of the three caretakers we had in Riverside Mansions. Bill Brown and Dick Powell were the other two. Charlie retired to live elsewhere, I believe.

These guys were great. Unlike council porters today, these blokes actually fixed things in your flat when they broke. They'd sweep the squares clean, unblock sinks and mend fuses and stuff. Their main role was to stoke the boilers with coke, which produced the hot water to the sinks and bathrooms in the flats. Something of a luxury at the time.

Come 9pm though, they would be out in force to clear all the kids from the open spaces and staircases, and woe betide you if you gave them any lip or failed to move on. They'd be round to see your Dad that night, and you'd get a wallop when you came in.

Charlie kept a nice garden, and we inherited a loganberry bush in the back garden. It never bore any fruit. Actually it did, but no one in our family ever saw that, as I used to get out there early, nick the berries and put them in my cornflakes before they could see them mature.

The three large open squares of the flats were great and we'd play in them for hours.

Team games like Run Outs, Hide and Seek, Tin-Can-Tommy, Cricket and 20 a-side football matches The football matches would come to a halt regularly whenever some old dear walked across the pitch with her shopping. Someone would shout "Freeze!" and everyone had to stand where they were until she got out of the way. That wouldn't happen today, would it?

With the "pea souper" smogs we used to get in London during the 1950's, we'd hide out in the open squares of Riverside and never get found. Whenever a game of hide and seek went on too long someone would restart the game by calling. " Ally, ally in. We're not playing, Cat's got the measles!" ...What was that all about?

Invariably, the organised games would break down into a disagreement over something but, never mind, Keith Brooks would always sort it out with his favourite saying. "According to the book of rules I've got upstairs..." He was a nice kid but could be a pain in the arse with his rules.

Sometimes we'd play football across the square instead of down the length of it. This was always a bit hazardous as the goals were then in front of the garden fences of the flats. Of course, the inevitable happened and I hit a screamer, which flew over the fence and broke through the front room window at the rear of a neighbour's flat. It was the Connolly's place. They are a boxing family and their Dad, Terry, was the guy who led the Wapping procession band. He used to wear a cap with feathers in I,t and used to toss the bandleader's stick high in the air and catch it every time. These were scary people to me.

Anyway, the window goes "crash" and everyone else legs it. Mr Connolly is now looking out of the broken window and I'm the only one standing there. I went home and told Mum and the two of us went to see him. I showed him my post office savings book and all the money I'd saved from my newspaper round and said I would pay for the repair. He thought I was cute, rubbed my head and said to forget all about it. I haven't to this day. He was a nice guy after all.

On cold nights, we kids would play in the "drying room", which was always incredibly warm. The Mums would take their wet washing to the drying room, which had these huge butcher-block type wooden tables in them. The Mums all had keys to open very long cabinets with horizontal poles inside them on which they would hang their bed sheets, etc. The waste heat from the boiler chimneys would dry the clothes. Environmentally friendly or what?

We'd play "Truth, dare, pluck, promise, kiss, command or opinion?" in there. This always ended up with the boys kissing the girls. You took turns in asking each other, say, "Do you have the pluck to kiss Lorraine Garland/Patty Simpkins/Beverley Gudge?' Then it was the girls' turn to ask each other the same questions about the boys, Joey Walsh, Robert and David Exley and Charlie Ruskin.

There was a derelict hospital in Wapping, called St George's-in-the-East. It housed hundreds of Hungarian political refugees after the uprising in the late 50s, and we grew up with rumours of rape, weapons, thefts and craziness. We couldn't understand them and they could not understand us. Sounds familiar? Could be England today, eh? Nothing's changed, just the nationalities.

We felt safe playing out in those days though, as no strangers came to Wapping. It was a scary place full of hard men, and it was also out of the way and not easy to get to. If you saw any strangers, you'd point them in the direction of the Prospect of Whitby pub before they'd even ask for it. It was the oldest Inn on the River Thames and world famous. Frank Sinatra and Judy Garland even came to it.

We kids used to scrounge money off the wealthy tourists who came to it in the flash cars. We'd run alongside the cars as they parked, open the doors, and salute them and say, "Look after yer car, Sir?" We'd always get a few coppers off them and, if they were rich, maybe a florin (10p).

As kids, we always looked forward to bonfire night on 5th November each year. We created the largest bonfires in London, I reckon. Well, certainly in East London, as we would travel far and wide to nick all the wood collected by other gangs of boys outside Wapping.

Playing on bombsites was a happy memory, but there was nothing happy about one particular bombsite memory I cannot ever forget; but I'll tell you about that later.

The area was still recovering from the Blitz, and the pickings were good in the old bombsites. Doors were our favourite as they were painted and went up in flames well. We'd go up to Watney St Market and nick a few fruit and veg hand carts, and then go up to, say, Matilda House, in Tower Hill, and we'd nick their bonfire wood. It was like a war, and they were the enemy, and we'd come home to Wapping with the spoils of war.

Freddie Ransome was, of course, the leader of the bonfire gang, too. The older boys had handed down the methodology of building huge bonfires over the years. We are talking 3 stories-high bonfires that only the fire brigade could put out. We'd relight them as soon as they left, by nicking petrol out of Yiddle Davis' lorry yard and using it to get the damp wood away again.

One particular year, I said I would buy myself one of those rockets that we used to see on TV at the start of "Sunday Night at the London Palladium" programme. This was a popular live TV variety show in the 1950s and 1960s.

I carried this rocket around with me all night and refused to light it until all my mates got bored with me and wanted to go home.

"Right…stand back" I say to the waiting crowd. "No… further back". "Oh, for fuck's sake, Exley, just light it," says Dennis Ayris, a mate who also lived in Riverside.

I'll show 'em, I thought. I placed this huge rocket into a tall, sterilised milk bottle and lit it, pushing the crowd back. There was a roar and the rocket started to take off.... It lifted all of 5ft from the floor, hovered for a few seconds then dropped to the floor and spat out two coloured balls of light before fizzling out entirely.

What a berk...the gunpowder had been spilling out of the rocket all night while I'd been carrying it around with me. They slaughtered me about it, and I was made to feel really stupid about it every November for years!

1962
When we go down Hopping...

*"We'd bring bed linen with us and fill it with fresh hay,
when we got there, to make mattresses and pillows".*

Summer holidays in Wapping back in the 1950's and early 60s were taken at local seaside holiday camps in Essex, or we'd go hop picking down in Kent.

Presumably, if Dad was skint, we'd go Hop Picking, because the adults were paid for doing that all day while we played in the fields, rode on the back of tractors, or went "scrumping" for apples and pears, raiding orchards for anything edible we could lay our hands on without being caught by the farmers.

The parents and older members of the family would set out for the hop fields in the morning and book themselves in with the farmers. Then they'd set themselves up under a vine, pull it down with a hop pole and strip the hops from it into a big canvas hopper and chat for hours and hours. At the end of the day, they would be paid by the bushels of hops they had collected and then spend the money in the pub that night.

We used to go to Cronks Farm in Yalding, in Kent, and stay in an old army nissan hut. Basically, the hut was formed of two brick walls at each end and an arched ceiling made from corrugated iron sheets. There was no electricity at all. We'd bring bed linen with us and fill it with fresh hay when we got there to make mattresses and pillows. There'd be a few gas lanterns for light at night, and we'd all sit round a campfire late into the night cooking apples in the fire and singing songs.

"When you go down hopping,
hopping dahn in Kent,
See old muvver Riley putting up 'er tent
With a t-i-o, a-t-i--o
A t-i-t-i-o

The site toilet facilities were dreadful. There was a tiny shack in the orchard, away from the hopping huts. Inside the hut was a bench with a large hole in it, over a trench full of shit and piss. You could only go into it with a bottle of Dettol disinfectant stuck up your nose.

Great times, though, and we always came back from hop picking with a rosy suntan.

If things were better, we'd go to Leysdown-on-Sea and stay in a chalet at the Vanity Farm holiday camp. The first thing I'd do is get myself a paper round with the local newsagent. Yes, it meant dragging a heavy sack full of newspaper round the campsites but it gave me a few bob to spend in the penny arcades and fun fairs without asking Mum and Dad for money.

We'd go to the beach in the daytime and go crab fishing later, off the promenade, when the tide came in. We'd fly kites in the afternoon and, after a bit of tea, we'd all go to the clubhouse where there would be some entertainment. Usually bingo followed up by a band of some sort - a drummer, a pianist, a guitarist and a singer.

All the kids on the campsite would have to stand outside the hall with a packet of crisps and a glass of lemonade or cream soda. We'd amuse ourselves by playing "Flying Angel" fights or something. This involved sitting on the shoulders of your brothers or sisters and tackling each other to the ground. Great fun.

We'd always end up on the dance floor at the end of the night singing to the tune of "Goodnight Sweetheart";

"Good night campers
See you in the morning
Good night Campers
Good night........."

Not too many people had cars in Wapping at the time, but Dad bought an old Foden van to get us to the seaside and back. We called it Nellie. It had been retrofitted with bus seats in the back of it, and had two large headlights that looked like eyes on the two steel mudguards over the front wheels.

Even our dog, Pepe, came on holiday with us.

Going to Jaywick Sands was fun, too. I can remember us queuing to get fagots and saveloys and chips on the way back from the clubhouse. I can still smell them now. One smell I also never forget, though, is the "Stinkeroo" man and his truck.

Once a week, everyone had to have an away day from the holiday camp. This was the day he came around to empty all the sewage that flowed from the chalets to the sewage tanks in the fields. Yuck!

These were lovely times and we were at our happiest when all seven of us were away on holiday together, even though it was only a few miles away from our East End home.

1964
Put your dukes up

"Suddenly you are in world of your own. The crowd is very noisy, but you can no longer hear them. It's like you are wearing ear defenders. There's noise, but it's not coming into your ears anymore"

I was keen on sports as a schoolboy and played cricket and football for the school before trying my hand at boxing. I entered the East London Schoolboy Championship and met the reigning champion in the first fight. He subsequently knocked the fuck out of me. I recall getting through the firstst round and, when I sat down in the corner, seeing four trainers in like a kaleidoscope formation. The second round did not last long and I got stopped for failing to defend myself!

I told myself that night that I would learn how to fight properly and I did.

In early 1964, I joined Broad St Amateur Boxing Club, a local Boxing club in Shadwell, and took up the Noble Art. Local dockers and business men ran the club. Bert Lilley was match maker and Harry Baynard was club secretary. My brother, Rob tried it too, but he didn't stick it out. Rob was a street fighter and a good one though. I wasn't much cop in the streets, but I found I could box well in the ring.

Boxers have to be disciplined, and there is quite a lot of protection provided by the Amateur Boxing Association (ABA). Before any fighter steps into the ring, he is weighed in and has to face a medical examination, which included a testicular examination, for ruptures, I suppose. Your ABA medical card is also inspected to see if an opponent had recently stopped you. If so, that would stop you from fighting for few months.

You are either matched well in advance of any bout and would appear in the programme or you'd turn up with your kit and be matched properly on the night. Novices only fight other novices until they are ready to step up to more skilled opponents.

If a match was made on a show, your name would be chalked up on a board back stage, so you would roughly know when you would be due to be gloved up before your fight.

It's then that you start looking around for someone your weight and age and, if you think you have worked out who your opponent is, you start to give him the evil eye in an attempt to look confident and to strike some fear in him.

The tensest moments are after you are gloved up and sitting ringside waiting for the fight before yours to finish.

After the bell to end that fight is rung…you get a sickening feeling in your tummy… your legs go weak and your mouth goes as dry as a desert.

Suddenly you are in world of your own. The crowd is very noisy, but you can no longer hear them. It's like you are wearing ear defenders. There's noise but it's not coming into your ears any more. Once you are in the ring, all you ever see is your opponent's eyes for the duration of the fight.

It's a surreal experience, it really is.

After a couple of exhibition matches (no winner or loser fights), I was down to make my full debut, away from Wapping, at Tilbury Amateur Boxing Club. The docks were still thriving and there was a great rivalry between the London and Tilbury Dockers.

Five of us from Broad St Amateur Boxing Club made our debut that night, all against local Tilbury boys. We all won and you can imagine how that went down with our Dads, who had built the club and erected the ring in the gym themselves. They all came along on the coach with us to cheer us on. Dad was extremely proud of me that night.

On Sunday mornings, we'd all train alongside British Champions, Henry Cooper, Dave Charnley and Terry Downes, in the pro gym at the Thomas a Beckett pub in the Old Kent Rd.

I'd fought about 10 times for the club that year and then met Tony Hafford, the East London Champion, again. This time, it was the semi-final. This was the boy who had soundly beaten me in the previous year's competition. I was giving him a good fight and looked like winning, when the ref suddenly stopped the fight and disqualified me for holding and hitting my opponent and low blows. I'd obviously picked up a few pro moves at the Thomas a Beckett since the previous year and the ABA did not approve of that behaviour.

Boxing definitely made me a better person as a young man. I understood very early in my life the importance of keeping fit, of fair play and how to say "better luck next time" when defeated. Mind you, I only ever said that 4 times.

My 2nd defeat was at a boxing show held by St Pancras Amateur Boxing Club. This was a huge event and the trophies were being given out by Sandie Shaw, a famous pop singer at the time from Dagenham who had hit records such as "Puppet on a string", "Girl don't come", "Always something there to remind me". Kenny Lynch, a mixed race pop singer/comedian from Stepney ("Up on the roof"), was also there, as well as Terry Downes, a former world champion boxer and ex U.S. Marine. Terry was now making films playing a hard man. He had a "distinguished" boxer's nose and gravelly voice. I would hear that voice throughout my fight that night.

I enjoyed meeting the stars that night and getting their autographs but I wasn't in great form and didn't start the fight well. I realised by the end of round two that I could not beat the guy in front of me, but I didn't want to lose badly or be stopped again. So I decided to defend myself well and get out a good loser on this occasion. Terry Downes was in full flow and cheering on the local boy. A little too noisily for my liking and, during one clinch with my opponent, I told him so.

"Why don't you just shut up, you prick "I called out to him. He just laughed and carried on. I didn't like him and have never forgotten that loss nor his rowdy behaviour.

The Broad St Amateur Boxing Club kit was cheap crap and we were always very envious of the St Pancras boys' kit. Jimmy Flint, a fellow "Wappingite" and one of the Broad St boys, nicked some of their kit that night from the dressing room. He also stole all the meal vouchers off the prize-giving table. Boxers used to get a free supper if we'd fought on a show. Jimmy got himself loads of Mars bars and crisps with the vouchers on the night and sold them to us.

He turned up for the next training session at Broad St in St Pancras' shiny shorts and we bought some from him too. He was a right little sod then.

I'm not sure I had the killer instinct required for boxing.

I can remember boxing one boy in particular, Charlie Wingrove from West Ham Amateur Boxing Club. It was the second flight we'd had and I was already one win up on him. This time we were fighting in his home territory, The Black Lion Pub in West Ham. He had all his mates and family in the audience too.

It's a small venue with a low ceiling. So, with the ring raised from the auditorium floor, you actually fought in a fog of cigarette smoke that formed at ceiling level. I was well on top; Charlie was struggling and desperate to win. He was coming after me when I slipped a jab from him and caught him right up "the bread basket" ....the belly.

He let out a huge whine that only I could hear above the crowd's cheering and he clung onto me. He had no wind left inside him at all. I could see the anguish in his eyes and the concern on the faces of his parents, sitting at ringside, over his shoulder.

This is where any real fighter, like Jimmy Flint, say, would go for the kill, but I chose to let him off the hook and I just saw the fight out, and was declared a unanimous winner by all three judges at ringside.

Another fight that stands out in my memory was when I was matched on a bill at Canvey Island Amateur Boxing Club.

I hadn't seen who I was to fight until I got in the ring and was a bit nervous because our trainer, Johnny Buckley (The Bermondsey Bomber), was not with us.

Bert Lilley, the club Secretary, was in my corner that night. I met my opponent in the centre of the ring to shake hands. "Fuck me", I said to myself. "He's got a fucking moustache!" He must have been much older than me as I did not then have any pubic hair.

He was a home boy and came out strong, chasing me around the ring trying to land one on me.

I was on my toes, bobbing and weaving and getting some retaliatory jabs into his face.

At the end of the first round, I came back to Bert and I said, "What the fuck have you done, Bert, putting me in with him; he's going to kill me. Look at all the badges on his shorts".

Bert said, "Don't worry about all that old bollocks. You're doing fine. Just keep jabbing and moving".

I'm now peering over Bert's shoulder at my opponent in the other corner and can see the ref has stopped the fight after the first round because I've cut his lip with my defensive jabs. "He only stopped it, Bert," I say with relief. "Don't be silly," he says, "You ain't doing that good".

"No, Bert, look, I've fucking won," I says. I meet the guy in the centre of the ring again for the result to be announced. He was not a happy bunny, but I was going home safe and sound again with another win under my belt.

I think I had a lucky escape that night in Canvey, though.

I boxed on the same bills as other kids that went on to be World Champions, boys such as John H Stracey and Maurice Hope, Charlie Magri. Johnny would win the Best boxer of the Night every show he was on. He was a very stylish boxer indeed.

To quote Marlon Brando from the film On the Waterfront, "I could have been a contender, Charlie!"

1965
Our world changes forever

"Your Dad died this morning Be good boys for me".

I always held my Dad in the highest esteem, but I never felt I could ever get on the best side of him. I don't ever remember him cuddling me or saying that he loved me. In fact, I'm not really sure if he even liked me.

Dad was a very strict disciplinarian. Some would say he was a very hands-on Dad. Let's be honest about this now, he was very heavy handed. He even kicked me under a table once while we were on holiday.

But, despite all that, he was still a hero in my eyes. He was a good-looking bloke who always looked smart on parade in his blazer, white shirt and tie and his grey flannel trousers. His shoes were so shiny you could see your face in them. I used to polish them for him on Sundays. One of his shoes had a thicker sole and heel than the other.

I never knew Dad without his severe limp. He was stricken with Arthritis in the hip and was always in severe pain. He had his shoes made up specially for him by Wolfie, the shoe repairman in King David Lane, a street that ran between The Highway and Cable St.

Dad was a very popular bloke amongst his fellow dockers and our neighbours. He liked a drink; most dockers did.

Dad had been a regular (in fact, a Sergeant) in The Army, as were his brothers, Monty and Danny. He served in the Royal Army Medical Corp, attached to the WAFF, the West African Frontier Force, in the 2nd World War. He was injured at the D-Day landings, and he was also there at Belsen, when the Alliance Forces liberated the starving Jews incarcerated in that concentration camp.

Like many of his time, he never really spoke about it.

But I loved hearing about the 2nd World War in the 50s and would buy 2nd hand Army surplus equipment, clothing, badges and medals from Petticoat Lane on Sundays. Many of these things still had blood on them and you could still smell the Brylcream in the RAF caps.

When Dad was out, I'd go through the drawers in his bedroom and sneak a look at the black and white photos of him serving overseas in the war. He had some photos of the dead Jews in Belsen. One was of a huge pile of naked, emaciated bodies.

Dad had a tough life and it was about to get even tougher.

He was diagnosed with cancer of the bowel around 1963 and had to have a colostomy bag fitted to his side to excrete into. I can still see him now perched on the edge of the settee in his favourite red woollen cardigan, the one with the brown leather football-like buttons and the two side pockets, cleaning his stomach wound and changing his colostomy bags, cursing his misfortune and the pain he was in.

So our home always smelt of something awful. It was either the waste from Dad's side or the Ralgex he would heavily apply to his severely painful arthritic hip. Mum would try to cover it up by overdoing the housework and applying more than a liberal use of Lavender furniture polish on all the walnut sideboards we had.

My poor Dad had five kids of school age, and it seems as though he was ill for as long as I ever knew him, what with his arthritis and his cancer. He never let it defeat him, though, and was always available for work in the docks and a few pints down the pub. He kept working right up to the last few weeks of his life.

He would sing Al Jolson songs, like "Mammie", or Frankie Vaughan songs, like "Gimme the Moonlight", at the drop of a hat, accompanied by Sid Robinson on the piano in Mooney's pub (The Three Suns) at the top of Garnet St.

Mum would say he spent far too long in the pub and there were always major rows when he came home. We'd sit at the top of the stairs, crying, just listening to them. I don't think he ever hit Mum. But he took his frustration out on us instead.

Dad became very sick and there was no more they could do for him. They put him in a Hospice but he wasn't religious and wanted to come home to die. He was still visited by the local convent nuns, who meant well.

Dad didn't want to see them and would call down from upstairs telling them to clear off. But they were on a mission to get him to heaven and did not let up. So they brought him broth every day and said they could tell Dad was in too much pain to see them and would just bless us and pray for us downstairs and leave.

I remember coming home every day from school for several months, almost forgetting about him during the day, but then, as I walked into the open square of the flats, I'd ask myself, "I wonder if me Dad died today?" The relief that he hadn't was enormous.

He finally died on 10th April 1965. I was just 13 years old, and it's a day I and my family never forget

Dad fell into a deep coma after our local GP came and gave him a heavy dose of Morphine to ease his increasing pain. He passed away in his sleep a night or two later.

The previous night he was dreaming he was reversing lorries into the Brussels Wharf dock entrance gates. "That's it, mate, keep coming, that's it". He'd been given light duties after he became ill. That job actually did for him, because he was going along ok for a while, and then a lorry in the yard hit him. We believed that started the cancer off again.

It was the silence after his deep comatose snores that woke Mum up that morning.

She didn't tell the youngest kids straightaway but let us sleep in while they took Dad away. Rob and I were having a pillow fight when she came into our room and just said "Your Dad died this morning. Be good boys for me".

We stopped playing, fell silent and made a bad job out of making our bed.

Dad was brought back a few days later and was laid out in the front room in his open coffin on two trestles with purple drapes over them. The windows and the telly were covered in white sheets and the mirrors were taken out of the room. There was a big candle lit on a side table.

I held our dog Pepe in the box room above the stairs while the brought Dad's coffin in. I remember them struggling to get him through the porch doors and banging the coffin against the walls and doors. "Don't you dare drop him", I said to myself and Pepe.

The coffin lid was removed and it stood against the wall above his head. There was a brass plaque on it with his name and his dates of birth and death inscribed on it. We were brought in to see him.

I was small then and I could only see his nose and eyebrows above the side of the coffin unless I stood on tiptoes. I did. He just looked asleep.

I wept a little in shock. I couldn't understand why Dad did not sit up in his coffin and tell me it would all be ok. I don't think Robert cried at all then, but he should have. It would have done him good.

I walked out into the square and across to the stone stairs of the flats to be on my own. My mate Charlie Ruskin's Mum must have seen me because she came down from the top floor and took me up to her Mother's flat where I broke down and cried like the child I was.

Charlie and his parents lived in Glamis Court, a real slum, two up two down dwelling with no bathroom. They lived in the two up bit and another family lived downstairs. A courtyard outside two rows of these terrace houses had a large open gutter running down it. Real Victorian stuff. They used to nickname these dwellings "Honeymoon Cottages" because that's where the young newlyweds in Wapping would live when they first got married until they could get somewhere better.

I suspect Charlie's Mum was in Riverside Mansions having a bath in Charlie's Nan's flat. She lived just a few doors away from where we used to live, in No.218.

We had many visitors in the days after Dad died; even Cardinal Heenan popped in while he was in the area and blessed Dad for us.

Several priests and nuns visited us in the days leading up to the funeral, and they kept changing their minds as to whether Cardinal Heenan could or could not make it. Last we heard was that he couldn't. So we were sitting around in the kitchen full of cups of tea, booze, half eaten sandwiches, etc., adults are standing around smoking themselves to death and filling the ashtrays when suddenly the priests burst in, shouting, "He's coming, he's coming".

So everything was cleared away to an upstairs bedroom and literally thrown onto the bed, all the kitchen windows were thrown open to clear the smoke and we all stood to attention as if a sergeant major was about to inspect an army barrack room.

In comes Cardinal Heenan himself and we all nod or curtsey in reverence and kiss his ring. All except my cousin Peter who is not aware of what he should do. The Cardinal puts out his hand and Peter shakes it firmly. "No, you should kiss my ring," says the Cardinal. Peter blushes and does.

We still tease Peter about the day he kissed the Cardinal's ring!

But the cremation that Dad always wanted caused some family problems on his side.

In fact, we saw hardly anything of them once he died.

What hurt most was that his sister (Aunt Bet) even used to walk across the square of our flats to visit her in-laws on the anniversary of their Dad's death.

She thought she was posh living in a council house in Dagenham!

They'd pass back across the square with bunches of flowers for his grave and she would have the same look on her face that the Queen has on Remembrance Sunday. Shame she couldn't remember my Mum and her burden.

I think the problem was that the Exleys were practising Catholics and a cremation was seen as a mortal sin by Dad's brothers and sisters. Dad always said he didn't want the worms to get him. We cremated him and so they couldn't.

Rob and I would meet Aunt Bet's husband in our local pub in Wapping about ten years after Dad died. He came up to Rob and says. "Hiya, it's me, your Uncle Dan!" I would have said hello but Rob, quick as a flash says. "I ain't got an Uncle Dan". We never saw them again for many, many years. Who cares, their loss.

I'll always remember the day of Dad's funeral. We couldn't find our little dog Pepe that morning. When we opened the front room door, there he was, lying half asleep under my Dad's open coffin, looking after his master.

The funeral procession took us past Dad's favourite pubs, the Jolly Sailor (Stewarts), and Mooneys and passed the Brussels Wharf dock gates where he'd worked. His mates came out and took their hats off. We couldn't cry any more now, which upset Mum.

The five of us kids were all still at school. Catherine was just 11, for Christ's sake, and too young to go to the funeral. She remembers that she preferred to play hopscotch with her friend. But she was never going to be allowed to go anyway.

When we got back home the neighbours had prepared everything and we had a traditional East End wake and a few drinks. I remember someone offering the funeral director, Alf Tadman, a plate of sandwiches, which he politely turned down. He wanted to get off to the next funeral, I suppose. We offered them to Pepe, as he would eat absolutely everything and anything. We pissed ourselves laughing as the dog took one sniff and ran off. We reckon he could smell the "hand of death" from Alf!

In the same year Dad died, the nation itself lost one of its heroes, former Prime Minister Sir Winston Churchill. I can remember going the river park to witness his coffin being brought up the Thames by a launch attended by riverboat men in their full garb.

The dockers manned their cranes on the wharves that day and lowered them as the launch passed along the river. What an amazing sight.

I later stood on the top floor balcony of Riverside Mansions to watch a large RAF fly past go over London.

School days, the best time of your life?

Charlie McKeown was a big Irishman who frightened the shit out of everyone. He was like the sports teacher in the film "Kes".

Rob and I were at St Gregory the Great Secondary Modern School in Bethnal Green when Dad died. Another school run by the Church. We'd swapped the wicked nuns in the junior school for wicked Christian Brothers by now. The Head Master, Br. Peter, was a nasty bastard. Baldy headed and with glasses, he could have been mistaken for Himmler, the Nazi. He'd punch you in the face if he did not have the cane to hand. He was ably assisted by his second in command who, for legal reasons, I won't name. He was another nasty bastard who used to touch the boy's bottoms, get an erection and expose his old lad to us daily.

I organised a petition about him and gave it in secretly to the head master. This was a big mistake. I was identified as an anti-Christ and was severely beaten for falsely accusing him. He was found out in the end, after I'd left school, and he was sent off to a retreat in the country somewhere.

Having failed the 11+ examination in Wapping, I couldn't go to St Bernard's grammar school, but went to St Gregory the Great Secondary Modern. But grammar schools were being done away with and all my old pals who had passed the 11+ later joined us "idiots" in a comprehensive school anyway when St Gregory's merged with St Bernard's.

Rob and I were put into different classes when that happened. The classes were divided into five streams based on the quality of the work you could produce. I was in Magellan, the middle stream, and he was in Nansen, one below us.

All the school dunces were put in Shackleton, one below Nansen. There were no special needs classes then.

There were two streams above Magellan and all the Wapping boys who had earlier passed the 11+ were put into them.

But at least the Wapping boys were all back in the school again. So we became even better friends, played league football together and subsequently went out drinking with each other in our teens and holidayed abroad as young men. That friendship lasts today as we approach our 60's

The new Comprehensive St Bernard's was spread across two sites in

Shoreditch and Bethnal Green. Local gangsters, the Krays, lived just down the street from the schools in Valance Rd (Fort Valance, as it became) and there was a bullet hole our Shoreditch school wall.

We had some good and some bad teachers in my secondary school. I had a lot of time for three in particular. Mr Shabarias a big, bald-headed Jewish guy - we never knew his first name, Jack Plant and Charlie McKeown.

Mr Shabarias refused to call me by my correct name and always called Huxley instead of Exley.

I'd object to this every day and he would call me out to the front of the class, throw a big arm around me, pretending to him me and say, " Look here, Huxley, I know who I'm talking to…you know who I'm talking to." Then he'd thump me on the back and send me back to my seat. We'd do this every day. He had some great sayings, too. He'd give us some work and say "Cobbler, cobbler, mend my shoe, get it done by half past two" and "Take your time…but hurry up!" When pointing at a map of the world, he would say,"here's Honna-on-the-loo loo" and "here's Winny-on-the-peg".

He was great fun.

Jack Plant would give you the slipper if you were naughty. It was actually the rubber sole off an old carpet slipper. He would chalk a swastika on it and he called it El Kabong, after someone in the cartoon Quick Draw McGraw. After he'd hit you with it, the swastika was transferred to the seat of your shorts! He smoked a pipe and scratched his balls a lot.

Charlie McKeown was a big Irishman who frightened the shit out of everyone. He was like the sports teacher in the film "Kes". He liked a bet and used to eat his breakfast toast in the class. He would take us to do sports out to Fairlop in Essex and would play football against us as if every game was the F.A. Cup Final.

He hit me once and I said I'd get my Dad on him. He told me to go and get him. It turns out he fought half a dozen Dockers when he taught in St Patrick's in Wapping many years earlier and he beat them all up.

I never did get my Dad on him.

I went back to see him 15 years after I left school and had a pint with him at lunchtime. He told me how he later found out the truth about the Brother who was exposing himself to us kids and he'd asked God to forgive him and his colleagues for the beating I got after I handed in my petition about that bastard so-called holy man.

The swinging 60's

*"Uncle Bill worked in the Royal Mint, by Tower Bridge.
He was a bit of a spiv. Well that's what Aunt Marge
called him. He used to smuggle me and Rob into
Hackney and West Ham dog tracks".*

London was the place to be now. It was the swinging 60's and we had the Beatles, mini-skirts, free love, the pill, and everything was changing. Man was in space and Cassius Clay was the World Heavyweight Champion.

I remember us getting our first telephone around this time. It was an avocado coloured handset with a circular dial on the front. I can still remember the number now. It was ROY 6485.

Until we got that, we had to use the red phone box that was on the corner of the street outside the Jolly Sailor pub. We'd tell friends to call us there at a certain time. If you got there and someone else was on call, it was ok to knock on the window and tell him or her to be quick.

I can also still remember the number of that call box. It was ROY 7110. The ROY stood for the name of the Royal Telephone Exchange. To make a call from one of these telephone boxes, you had to lift the receiver, put in four pennies and push button A when you got through. If you didn't get through, you pressed button B to get your coins back. If I ever passed a call box as a kid, I'd pop in and press button B just in case someone else had forgot to. I invariably got some money to drop out. Sounds like million years ago, eh?

There were no pop programmes on TV for young people but we could hear pop records on Radio Luxembourg. Well sort of. We had a radio perched at high level on a shelf that used to have a gas meter on it. We connected a cable from the aerial socket to the gas pipe to get the best reception. However, the signal from Luxembourg would notoriously fade in and out entirely every minute or so. So we would usually hear either the start of the Beatles latest record or the end of it, or sometimes miss it entirely if it was a short song.

We had similar problems with the signal for the telly, and invariably one of the kids had to stand there with the portable TV aerial in their hand over their head while the rest got to see Gun Smoke or Z cars or whatever was on.

Satellite TV was in its infancy then and Dad would wake us up at 3:30am in the morning to watch Cassius Clay fighting his World title fights. We'd all sit around waiting for the satellite to pass over America and the pictures would start flickering into our set.

We'd do the same to watch American astronauts orbiting the Earth in space.

My Uncle Wilf and Uncle Bill were kind after Dad died, and in 1966 they took me to see Cassius Clay fight Henry Cooper for the World Heavyweight Title at Highbury Stadium.

Uncle Bill was married to one of Dad's sisters, Auntie Margie. They had just the one child (Julie) and they lived in the top half of a terraced house in Lefevre Rd in Bow.

Uncle Bill worked in the Royal Mint, by Tower Bridge. He was a bit of a spiv. Well, that's what Aunt Marge called him. He used to smuggle Rob and me into Hackney and West Ham dog tracks. He taught us how to use the Tote and pick the best dogs out. We used to really like him. He was always great fun to be with.

He reckoned if a dog had a piss on the parade at the start it was a good sign. Even better if it had just had a crap. It would be lighter, see, and would run faster. We believed everything he said too.

My cousin, Julie Wassmer, is now a writer for the TV soap East Enders.

Mum's sister, Auntie Eileen, lost her husband, Johnny Rigaluth, around the same time as my Dad died. They both got a reasonable payout from the Docks, the Union and the insurance and then decided they needed a change of life. Late in 1965, they bought a commercial business called The Washington Hotel, in Wellington Street, in Stockton on Tees, County Durham. Eileen had met a chef named Dave while working at a holiday camp, and they decided to go into business together. We kids were not part of that decision and just did as we were told and moved up North.

I'd lost touch with the schoolboy crush, Kathleen, by now. Moving to Stockton finished any hope I had of being with her for the rest of my life and that was hard to accept at the time.

The hotel was ok in itself. But it was odd to go from a small maisonette in Wapping to such a big house, with tens of bedrooms and bathrooms and a large dining/sitting room for guests.

I can't remember too much about it now.

I do remember a fellow calling for Mum one night saying, "Get yer walker on, we're going to the Mucky Duck". Apparently that's Geordie talk for "Put your coat on, we are going to the White Swan pub".

Rob and I were teased mercilessly at our new school because of our Cockney accents. Even the teachers would do it.

I hated every single day I spend in Stockton and, even more so, the time I spent in Mill Lane School up there. Auntie Eileen's new husband, Dave Bozeate, drove us kids mad trying to control us. "Don't defy me!" he'd shout. He was probably a really nice bloke, but he was not our Dad and never could be. We called him "Don't-Defy-Me Dave".

We used to play "up the wall" at school playtimes in Stepney. This entailed tossing coins at a wall to see who got closest. The winner could then toss all the coins in the air and could keep all those that fell heads upwards. This was a game of skill (even the tossing bit) and you could earn a few bob gambling any loose change you had.

These wallies at the school in Stockton used to rush from the classroom and claim a section of wall shouting, "This is my alley". Rob and I thought, great we'll skin them for their money.

Then they got out their bags of marbles and competed against each other for them. Same game as we played in Stepney but no money it. We'd look at them and say, "So what's the point of it?" "You win more or even better marbles", they'd reply. "Yes, but what's the point of that?" Stupid Northerners, we thought.

I wrote a letter from Stockton to my childhood sweetheart, Kathleen, to tell how much I was missing her. I don't remember getting a reply. I bumped into her again many years later and she told me she still had my letter and the valentine cards I'd sent her, which was really sweet. Perhaps the love I had for her as a kid was not as one-sided as I'd thought.

I joined the local Marine Cadets in Stockton with a school friend, Fred Douglas, just because they had a boxing club there. Rob had to be different and he joined the Sea Cadets. I turned up with all my flash boxing kit only to find everyone else dressed in 1930's Army-style sportswear. I had my own gloves, leather skipping rope and satin shorts, which did not go down well at all with the local scruffs.

"Come on then, Cassius Fucking Clay, let's have it in the ring". All ten of my new club-mates challenged me. These were bigger and older kids but I took them all on for a round each. I was getting more and more exhausted as each new opponent stepped in the ring to try to knock me out. I survived and hoped they would give me a bit of respect now.

No chance. When I went to school the next day, a queue of even bigger and older kids were waiting for me, all wanting to see me up on The Moors after school. That evening as school finished, they all turned right for The Moors and I turned left with Rob and went back to the Hotel. I don't think we went back to the school after that. Our older brother, Johnny, had stayed in London in 6 Riverside as he was working by then. Thank God he did, because we kids couldn't get on with living in Stockton at all, and Mum and her kids came home to where we belonged, back to 6 Riverside Mansions, Wapping in East London

1966
The World Cup and all that

"Some people are on the pitch," said BBCTV
commentator Kenneth Wolstenhome.
"They think it's all over... it is now!"

Rob and I used to go to watch Millwall FC on Saturdays in the early 60's. They were in the 3rd Division (South) at the time. There was no 4th Division then. This was because the teams at that end of the football league were so poor they couldn't afford to travel the length and breadth of the country, so they just played the local teams

We loved going to The Den, Millwall's football ground.

We'd get there early and play around on the level crossings and railway sidings in that part of South London. We loved the notoriety of Millwall FC and the fact they were crap did not bother us at all.

We'd stand next to away supporters and argue that we had the worst team not them. In later years it became more tribal and you'd fight anyone who said anything bad about your team

It would have been easy to support West Ham, Arsenal or Spurs but we didn't want to. Millwall were our nearest team and they came from the Isle of Dogs in East London originally, so there you go.

In the early days, we'd collect china teacups at half time and get the deposit back on them. It would pay for the fare home from New Cross Gate in South London back to Wapping on the other side of the Thames.

But if we timed it right on the way home, we could call the lift down at Wapping Underground Station and run up the stairs, poking our tongues out at the ticket collector in the lift as he passed us going in the opposite direction.

"I'll have you next time you little bastards," he'd shout. We weren't bad boys. Just cheeky sods, maybe.

Rob and I watched all of the 59 home games without defeat as Millwall set a record back in 1964/65 and then we started travelling the country with the away supporters as well.

Yes they were the worst behaved thugs you ever saw and I'm not proud of many of the things I witnessed. I've seen rapes on trains, knifings, everything. But I tell you if you were travelling to an away ground to see Millwall at the age we were, you'd put yourself in the middle of that pack for your own protection from the other team's hooligans, believe me.

In 1966, the World Cup Finals was coming to London. And we were all glued to our black and white TV screens watching Alf Ramsey's England team, led by West Ham's immaculate Bobby Moore, making their way through the final rounds.

16 teams from around the world had fought their way through the qualifying rounds over the previous couple of years. England, the host country, and Brazil, the previous winners in 1962, went straight into the finals. The 16 teams were divided into four groups of four. The top two teams in each group advanced to the quarterfinals. England, West Germany, Brazil and Italy were seeded into each of the four groups.

England finished top of Group 1 with only four goals to their credit, but had none scored against them. We went on to meet Argentina in a sour game that saw Rattin, the Argentinean Captain, sent off. Geoff Hurst from West Ham took injured legend Jimmy Greaves's place and scored a fabulous header to put England through to meet much fancied Portugal in the semi-final.

Manchester United's Bobby Charlton scored two great goals against Portugal's solo penalty goal from Eusebio, the tournament's best player.

Amazingly, on 30th July 1966, England found themselves in the final, on home turf at Wembley Stadium.

Rob and I had a paper round in the City of London. We'd go up on the number 15 bus with Mum before we went to school. She'd do her cleaning job in the offices and we'd deliver newspapers

We used to pick up bundles of newspapers from the various Fleet St. print works on sack trolleys and take them back to the newsagents, and, from there, deliver them to the barristers' offices in the Inns of Court and other offices in the area.

On the morning of the World Cup Final, I picked up my £3 wages and decided to go to Wembley on my own, thinking I could buy a ticket from a tout outside the stadium.

I arrived very early and the ticket tout prices were 3 times the face value, but I could buy a 10/- (50p) ticket for 30/- (£1.50p) and still get change for a programme and a hamburger. Try buying such a ticket today; somehow I don't think you'd get one for half the value of a kid's paper round eh?

I was one of the first in the ground and watched it fill up before kick-off at 3pm.

I'm surrounded by a mixture of Germans, English and, come to that, many other nationalities from around the world. I'm in a pen right above the player's entrance to the pitch. The Grenadier Guards had finished marching up and down the pitch before the game and were now resting on a balcony above the player's entrance directly below me.

It had been raining but, just before kick-off, it stopped and the sun started to come through.

Suddenly a big roar goes up. The fans at the other end of the pitch can see the players are in the tunnel below me.

The whole stadium goes crazy as the two teams walk out in lines. It took a while for me to work out who was who, as England were in red shirts and West Germany were wearing white, something I was not ready for, as England had always played in white till now.

Her Majesty Queen Elizabeth II, dressed in yellow from top to tail, takes her seat. A few seats away sat Harold Wilson, the Labour Prime Minister. Was this why we were playing in red shirts, I wonder!

West Germany kicks off and it's not long before we go one down and our hearts sink. Helmut Haller scores at the opposite end to me after 12mins and 32 seconds, but Geoff Hurst equalises at my end just a few minutes later.

In the second half, the game is starting to look like being a 1-1 draw when Geoff Hurst picks up the ball to the left, after a corner. What's he doing out wide, we all want to know? He centres and the ball is deflected high in the air causing some confusion in the German defence. Martin Peters and Jack Charlton are both homing in on the end of this looping deflection."For God's sake leave it to Martin, Jack", someone close by me shouts. He does and Martin volleys it straight into the net.

"England, England" chants the whole stadium.

With just seconds to go to the end of the normal ninety minutess Jackie Charlton, our magnificent centre half, towers over one of the Germans and concedes an unnecessary free kick. It's in exactly the same place that Bobby Moore took the free kick for Geoff Hurst to score our first half equaliser.

The ball is centred and bounces off a few players, and then drifts into free play again to the right hand side of the goal. Everything seems to be moving in slow motion as Wolfgang Weber slides in to put the ball past Ray Wilson and Gordon Banks to equalise.

By the time we kick off again, the game is over and we are now facing extra time.

Everyone is looking at each other in disbelief on the terraces. It had been a long fortnight of the finals and it's taking its tolls on the England team who are laid out on the pitch.

You have to remember that there were no substitutes in those days. You started with eleven players and, if you lost one, you continued with ten.

Manager Alf Ramsey is telling them "You've won it once, now go and win it again".

The game was under way again, with two halves of 15 minutes each way of extra time.

Eight minutess into the first half of extended play, Alan Ball is chasing onto a loose ball over to my left, he clips it into Geoff Hurst's path, but Geoff has his back to the goal and there is nothing on for him. He swivels on the spot to shoot, falling onto his back as he does so. The ball famously hits the underside of the bar and comes down on the goal line before being hit out of play by a West German defender. Roger Hunt of Liverpool turns away in celebration and Geoff gets to his feet claiming a goal.

Alan Ball runs to the linesman and so does the ref. The linesman, sporting a large tummy and matching moustache, nods his head and we all go potty as the ref points to the centre spot to declare the ball had crossed the line and it is a goal!

The tension is incredible and we just want the game to end now and England to win 3-2.

We are into the last minute, a West German attack breaks down and Bobby Moore has the ball in his own goal area. Jackie Charlton is screaming at him to just hit it up the other end of the pitch to waste some time. Supporters are running onto the pitch as the ref has his whistle in his hands and he is staring at his stopwatch.

Bobby ignores Jack Charlton and elegantly dribbles it out of his own area, past two Germans before making a fantastic forty-yard pass to put the ball ahead of - guess who? - yep, Geoff Hurst, again.

Geoff knocks it forwards a couple of times before throwing his left foot at the ball in the hope it will end up high in the stands. It doesn't. He hits it sweet and the ball flies into the top of the left hand corner of the net with poor Hans Tilkowski rooted to the spot again.

"Some people are on the pitch," said BBCTV commentator Kenneth Wolstenhome. "They think it's all over...it is now!

What a fantastic time I had and I came home to Mum about 6pm. "Where've you been son" she said casually. It was not unknown for me to be out all day on a Saturday.

"I've been to the World Cup Final Mum and we won 4-2", I say with a croaky voice.

"That's nice, son, but you'd better eat your tea before it gets cold"!

You have to remember, of course, that I couldn't call Mum on my mobile phone and tell her what I was up to, because they hadn't been invented then and, at that time, we did not have a land line in our home either.

One of the best moments at Millwall was when we drew Tottenham Hotspur at home in the 3rd round of the FA Cup in 1967. Spurs had a team full of Internationals and we were just a poor 3rd Division side.

It was going to be hard to get tickets for this one, so I decided to stay overnight outside the ground the night before they went on sale. I got there at 10pm and there were already a thousand people there with the same idea.

We all slept in the road with blankets; some had flasks of tea and passed them around. Hamburgers were on sale too.

We woke in the morning to find the queue had stretched down the road behind us all, but we were at the front and sure to get the one ticket that was being allocated per person. I got mine and, just as I left the ground, the police let the next couple of hundred fans into Cold Blow Lane, so I turned around as they passed me and got Robert a ticket too.

We went to the game and had never seen anything like it. The terraces were "standing only" at that time and there were 46,000 people recorded to be at the game, a ground record. I reckon there could have been 55,000 because fans were paying at the turnstiles and the blokes managing them were taking cash and telling them to jump over the turnstiles and pocketing the dosh.

Rob and I had to sit on edge of the pitch with all the other kids, as the crowd was so large. The linesman had to run up and down on the pitch itself. It was crazy.

We held Spurs to a 0-0 draw and went to White Hart Lane for the replay in mid-week and got beat by a goal carved out between Alan Gilzean and Jimmy Greaves. It was no disgrace at all as Spurs went on to beat Chelsea in the final.

1966
Our first holiday as the lads

*"We'd wondered what the strange whistling sounds
were. These were live rounds rifling past our heads!"*

We first holidayed without our parents as young chaps on a campsite in
Dover; we were just 15 years old and a bit naïve. The five of us put up a
tent in a field and then went off to the beach. We didn't fancy any spiders
coming into the tent, so we made sure the ground sheet extended beyond
the tent base. This was not a good move and we were flooded out after
a big downpour later that night and ended up sleeping in the communal
toilets instead!

This was nothing compared to what happened to us on our next visit
to the beach. Having walked as far as we could long the beach, the tide
came in and we were trapped on the beach. No problem, we can climb
The White Cliffs of Dover!

We did this ok by zigzagging our way up the cliff. But when we got to
the top we were faced with a row of large numbers (0-9). They were also
back to front. We did not know what this meant at all and just walked
across the field at the top of the cliff.

As we did this, we spotted a concrete army bunker. The coast was full of
these installations, so we weren't particularly bothered to see this.

As we reached it an Army squaddie leapt to his feet and pulled the four
of us to the ground. It turns out we were walking across a firing range and
the squaddie's job was to halt the shooting if a ship at sea went past the
cliffs.

We'd wondered what the strange whistling sounds were. These were
live rounds rifling past our heads!

We had one more holiday as schoolmates before we started work
proper, and we went to Leysdown. It was me, Rob, Charlie Ruskin, Dennis
Cochlin and Jimmy Duncombe. Jimmy was a protestant lad and a scout,
but he was all right. Charlie and I had to share a double bed, Rob took the
settee and Jimmy and Dennis were in the other double bed. Jimmy wasn't
keen on sharing a bed with Dennis and took a sleeping bag with him and
set it up on the top of the bed. He said he was wearing it in for a camping

trip. But we knew he was a bit shy about being in bed with another bloke.

We met up with a crowd of girls who thought we were cool and called us "The five tasty geezers from Wapping".

We would all get pissed and go to the beach at night, listen to the illegal pirate pop radio stations broadcasting from ships off the coast and swim in the sea with our clothes on. Simon and Garfunkel's Mrs Robinson was No 1 at the time.

There were strange illuminated sea urchins/jelly fish bobbing around in the sea; they actually emitted a light from within them. We would spend all night in the waves trying to catch them. We called them "the Blue Meanies" just like the strange beings in "Yellow Submarine" the full-length cartoon film that The Beatles had created.

I was lucky enough to be working in the West End of London on the night it premiered and I joined the crowd in the rain outside The London Pavilion in Piccadilly Circus to actually see The Fab Four arrive for the premier.

They pulled up in vintage Rolls Royces. I can remember Paul was all in black but George was in a tangerine suit with a matching floppy hat.

1967
Time to earn a crust

*"You would never make an electrician as long as you
had a hole up your arse". I did, though, and more.*

The Docks were closing in London. The work was literally going down
river. Container ships were the future and the Wapping dock basins
had been built for sail and could not cope with the deeper and longer
container vessels. I did not want to work in The Royals or, God forbid,
have to travel down to Tilbury Docks where the container port was being
created.

There were few men in Wapping who did not actually work in the
docks. One of them was Phil Coffey. He was always smartly dressed
on weekdays and he came to our flat from time to time and fixed any
electrical problems we had for a drink (a few bob on the side).

I used to watch him with his tool kit, fuse wire and stuff and thought it
was magical. Dad had given me an electrical shock with one of his wiring
repairs to the Christmas tree lights and I vowed then to learn more about
electricity before he killed me. The fact that you could earn a bit on the
side, like Phil, also appealed to me.

So Mum and I went along to the London Electricity Board to see a film
about a young man becoming an apprentice electrician. It was fantastic
and even had the Pathe News presenter, Bob Danvers-Walker, narrating
it. It's his voice you always hear narrating old black and white news items
over film clips from the 1960's.

It showed little Johnny turning up at a building site, to be met by the
foreman who gave him a donkey jacket and a tool kit and took him around
the site, introducing him to all the workers. They shook Johnny's hand
and took care of him and, by the afternoon, Johnny was installing socket
outlets. That will do for me, I thought, but I was in for a bit of shock as
this was not quite like the average building site or the workers on them.

I joined a small electrical firm near Kennington Oval called Leaf and
Carver Ltd, and started work on a building site in Finsbury Circus in the
City. I remember continuously falling over all the plant and debris on
the floor.

I was put to work with one of the most miserable bastards I've ever come across. He told me everyday how useless I was and how "You would never make an electrician as long as you had a hole up your arse". I did, though, and more. But no thanks to you, Ron!

I can't remember why, but I was moved from smiler Ron to a site in Hendon. It was a luxury block of flats called Holly Mount. The only luxury thing I could see was the waste disposal unit below the sink.

I was working with a bloke from Camberwell called Barry Wynn. He was a flash bastard with a Cortina. Well, he thought he was flash, but I thought he was just a prick from South London, but we got on. I learnt to play poker and had my first serious drinking experience that Christmas Eve in 1967. I came home so pissed that I could not get out of bed until Boxing Day and vowed never to touch whisky again, and I didn't for 25 years.

The site was full of flash bastards and none more flash than the lift engineers. They took great pleasure in beating me up or targeting me with a pellet gun thing we used to make on site. It was like a peashooter, but you shot putty instead. One of them got me right in the eye once and I vowed to get them back.

I got my chance when the two of them were working in the bottom of the same lift pit and I was working in a flat on the 5th floor in same block. The flats were set out in separate blocks with a common entrance, a lift bank and staircase in each. There were also adjoining rear balconies, so that tenants could escape a possible fire by stepping over the balcony to the next block and make their way out via another staircase.

This was an integral part of my cunning plan.

As the site was in its earliest state of development, there was nowhere for the site workers to have a piss. But there were piss buckets left around the site, which were emptied by a little Ethiopian labourer once a day. You've guessed it; the piss bucket was on 5th floor, right by the open lift shaft.

So I made a right show of myself at the ground floor to the lift boys, who told me to fuck off. Which I did. But as I left, I went to the block next door, climbed the stairs to level 5 and emptied the piss bucket onto them down the lift shaft!

I vaulted the balcony again and made my way down the stairs at the speed of light and walked into the ground floor again just as these two flash 'arrys were staggering out of the lift shaft covered in piss.

They couldn't blame me, could they! I laughed all the way home and could never keep a straight face whenever I saw them after that. You don't fuck with a Wapping boy and get away with it.

Leaf and Carver were struggling a bit and they made Barry redundant. He couldn't believe it as he had done his time (apprenticeship) with them. I didn't want to wait around for that to happen to me, so I started to look around for another job.

I joined Trollope and Colls Electrical Ltd. My brother John knew a "deaf and dumber" (plumber) with them. He gave me their telephone number and I got myself an interview with them. Mum came along with me to the interview and together we signed the "Master and Apprenticeship" indentures (I still have them to this day), and I spent 13 very happy years with Trollopes.

1967
The lads go abroad for the first time

"At that time General Franco was still in charge of
Spain and it was under military control. Anne and I
were having a midnight snog on the beach one night
and suddenly there was a border control soldier in jack
boots and a shiny three cornered hat prodding me in the
arse with his machine gun."

Robert, Charlie Ruskin and Dennis Cochlin and I were the first of the Wapping lads to travel abroad. It was 1967 and package holidays were in their infancy; we booked 10 days full board on the Costa Brava for £25. Well, I say 10 days; we flew across the Channel in a large plane with propellers on it and then it would take us a day and half to get to Spain by coach across the length of France.

We hadn't really planned for the long coach trip at all and thought we'd just sleep through that bit. We didn't even take any French currency with us.

By the time we got to the Pyrenees, we were stealing bread and milk from local town doorsteps to get something to eat.

The coach broke down at one point, in some remote part of France, and could not be repaired, so we had to hang around for a replacement. When it eventually came, it did not have enough seats. So, being the youngest on the trip, we volunteered to use the temporary seats. This involved pulling the two arm and head rests of the aisle seats out and making them into another. The only problem was if you moved they would spring back again and leave you on the floor of the aisle.It was the most uncomfortable 8 hours travelling ever and we got no thanks from all the old gits who were able to snore their way overnight to Spain. Actually, I'm glad I stayed awake, otherwise I would have missed seeing the amazing sight of the drivers changing over places while still driving at 70 miles an hour!

Spain was like a breath of fresh air compared to England at that time. All night Disco's, great music and fun, fun, fun. Even the beer different. It was called Lager and we brought some back to show our mates!

There was no going back to holidays in England again after this.

I met a lovely red haired girl from Streatham out there. I asked her name and she said. "Anne...with an E". So I called her Anne...with an E for the next 10 days.

At that time General Franco was still in charge of Spain and it was under military control.

Anne and I were having a midnight snog on the beach one night and suddenly there was a border control soldier in jackboots and a shiny three-cornered hat prodding me in the arse with his machine gun. "Get off the beach, Senor" he said. We did, and fast. The holiday was great value for money so we did it all again the two following years. We had to sign a government V form to declare that we were not taking more than £25 out of England. Fat chance. I took £15 and couldn't spend it all because it was so cheap in Spain at that time.

We came back on the coach absolutely skint one year and stopped just outside Paris to stretch our legs and grab a cup of coffee. Together the four of us didn't have enough for a large coke but we did have enough for two coffees. I thought, we can all have half a cup, right? So, as I had picked up a little French at St Bernard's school, the lads asked me to order. "Deux cafes, s'il vous plait", I says. I get a quizzical look from the waiter. He returns with two of the tiniest cups you'll ever see in your life. I should have said "Deux cafes au lait", of course, to get large coffees made with milk. We went outside and stole bread and milk from the doorsteps again.

Anne and I saw each other for several months. Her family were quite posh and had a lovely big house and I was out of my league with her. I couldn't afford to travel to Streatham at the time and we broke up.

1968
Mods and Rockers

"... there was Rob standing over the rocker. He'd chinned
him because he had the audacity to overtake him and
had also given him a dirty look."

Young men tended to fall into two distinct style groups in the 1960s. You were either a mod or a rocker. Mods were well groomed and rode shiny 200cc motor scooters and Rockers were more rough and dirty looking and rode powerful 650cc motor bikes. We both had different musical preferences too. Mods were into black Soul, Rhythm and Blues, Tamla-Motown music or London based groups such as The Kinks. Rockers were still stuck in the 1950's and would listen to Elvis Presley and Bill Haley and the Comets.

I was a Mod during my apprenticeship and I had a tonic mohair suit, hand-made by the Jewish tailor, Ron Artus, in Whitechapel for 36 guineas. (A Guinea being £1 and 1 Shilling). Quite a lot of money at the time. That suit and tie was my only protective clothing when it came to riding out on my scooter!

Mods didn't wear motorcycle helmets, either. It would have messed our hair up.

I had a terrific scooter. We'd drive up and down Roman Road all night on them. Rob had a Lambretta to be different. Mine was a post-box red GS 160 Vespa with a skimmed head, whatever that meant. It had chrome side panels, wheel arches and tool box, white wheels and loads of lights and mirrors. It had red tassels on the handles and a long whippy aerial with a fake tiger's tail hanging from it. I looked like a real tasty geezer on it.

I never took a test, so, if I pulled a sort (girl), I'd just take off my L-plates and get to her sit behind me anyway.

Rob couldn't stand Rockers at all. I remember driving up Garnet St one day and when I got to the T-junction with The Highway at the top; a Rocker sped past closely followed by Rob.

I turned right and followed them. When I turned the corner at the Rotherhithe Tunnel, there was Rob standing over the rocker. He'd chinned him because he had the audacity to overtake him and had also given him a dirty look. Rob got us into lots of bovver in our teenage years. He thought I was a chicken because I didn't like to get involved in fights in pubs, etc. But I did my fighting in the ring in front of hundreds of people, and the best man always won, not the hardest.

I remember shooting off home early from work one night and rushing through the City of London at 4:15pm on my Vespa. I had the words "Dave", and "Wapping" emblazoned on my mod parka and the bike itself and was easily recognisable.

The lights were just about to change ahead of me from green to red and I'd made a decision to risk it, when one of the Trollope and Colls "walking foreman" suddenly appeared in the middle of the crossing as the light changed.

It was Ernie Goldsmith, a right stickler for time keeping.

I couldn't stop or he would clean me for leaving site early, especially as I had handed my "crime sheet" (time sheet) to him that Friday morning showing a 5:30pm finish in Knightsbridge!

Ernie and I did our best to miss each other, dodging left, then right, and then left again. I missed him by inches and had to face a grilling the next week when I went into the office with the site crime sheets again. I just denied it was me and said must have been some other mod called Dave because I was "working until 5:30pm in the West End, Ernie, honest, mate".

Freddie Ransome was still seen as the leader of the gang. But Freddie came a cropper right outside Riverside one night. He was showing off by speeding down Garnet St past the Jolly Sailor. On his last run, a car poked its front bumper out of Prusom St. Freddie clipped it and was thrown across the road and rammed under the huge steel gates of the entrance to a warehouse on the other side of the road. His leg was broken in several places and he carries a limp with him today.

He was luckier than our friend Alan Wazny. He was the son of a Polish immigrant and had two brothers, Mark and Roy.

Alan was a rocker, but, because he lived in Riverside, he was not given a hard time. In fact, he was one of us.

Alan sadly died after falling under a lorry from his motorcycle at the top of Garnet St as he turned onto the Highway.

There was a Ready-Mix concrete batching plant at the bottom of Garnet St and, as the Lorries turned onto the Highway, they would always shed a few pebbles on the road. Alan's bike skidded on them and he lost his life at 19 years of age. We all gathered at his flat, No 101 Riverside, after the funeral. Mods and Rockers united as one, and we had one hell of a party to celebrate his young life.

Roy was a poof. Sorry, but that's what we called homosexual men in those days. The word Gay meant happy or cheerful then.

I suppose it was odd to find a man of his persuasion being totally accepted in the tough community we were growing up in the late 60s, early 70s, but he certainly was.

He used to come and watch our football team play to cheer his brother Mark on. Even in the pouring rain over Hackney Marshes, Roy would be there on the line under an umbrella.

One day, we were short of a full eleven and it was a big game, so we asked him to turn out for us. He couldn't play football but we just told him to stand on the wing and try to get in the way of their full back.

Roy played the whole game on a muddy pitch, mincing around under his umbrella and his kit was as clean at the end the game as it was at the start. We won and he must have contributed something. We did laugh when we all got back to The Jolly Sailor that Sunday lunchtime.

1967–1980
The Trollopes era

*"The faster the slide moved, the more bonuses we got;
the higher the slide got, the more danger money we got"*

I actually had several roles with Trollopes. Apprentice Electrician, Electrician, Approved Electrician (foreman). There were two separate sides to the electrical division.: the Construction Site Services side, which provided all the temporary lighting, power and plant to erect buildings, and the Electrical Installation fit-out side, which installed the permanent wiring into those premises.

I also went on to become an Air Conditioning Engineer with the firm.

The Electrical Installation side was full of good old boys that had been with them for years. Nice men, mostly, and I learned how to do a good job thanks to them.

I was about 17 when I started working with "Evil Sam" Milan who was just as miserable as Ron, my first electrician at Leaf and Carver. We carried out new installations in some of the older banks in the City. Some still had the very earliest forms of passenger lifts in them. You got in the lift as it was moving past the floor you were on. No doors or push buttons. These lifts were operated by hydraulics. There was a rope that passed straight through the lift car roof and floor. Pull the rope down and the lift went up, and vice versa. You could touch the lift shaft as the lift slowly rose or descended. As it approached the floor you wanted, you held the rope and the lift car slowed to a stop as you manipulated the rope to get the lift level with the landing. Sound bizarre now, doesn't it?

I later went off to work with John (Chalkie) White; he was an Arsenal fan but he and I got on. He had a brother, Keith, who was also a Trollopes apprentice. I could not stand to be in the same room as him and vice versa. He was a right goody-goody, and he didn't like me because I was an East Ender and a Millwall fan to boot. I always did whatever I could to upset Keith.

Chalkie blew it big time on one job we were assigned to do in an occupied office block near St Paul's Cathedral. We somehow caused a mains fuse in an occupied office block to blow at about 5:30pm one Thursday night.

I was working on the floor below Chalkie. We were pulling some new wires through from one floor to another and I was suddenly plunged into darkness. So was Chalkie. He told me to look for a blown fuse. But the fuses were a special cartridge type without any visible fuse wire as such. I thought I'd correctly identified it, so I pulled it out of the fuse board and made my way through the darkness up to him. The only light I could see was coming through a keyhole on what must have been a door to the outside world.

I opened the door and burst out into the street, only for the burglar alarms to operate. Two security guards spotted me standing there and they ran back into the building. Anyway, the old bill (Police) turns up and Chalkie and I had some explaining to do.

The problem now was that the security guards had re-set the alarm and Chalkie and I could not go back in.

"Don't worry, Chalkie", I reassured him. "I'll take the fuse into the workshop first thing in the morning and get another and we'll have it all sorted out by 9 am".

So I take this great big cartridge fuse home overnight and go into our Christopher St. stores in the morning. The guy in the stores tests it out and says there's nothing wrong with it.

Ooops! This means two things. There's still another big blown fuse in the building and we have also killed the power to another large part of it by pulling out the wrong fuse.

I arrived back at the building on my Vespa scooter and there is a big crowd outside it. Blokes with top hats on too. Stock Market chaps. They were not too happy about being taken off the markets by a couple of tossers like me and Chalkie.

We sorted it out but there was hell to pay for it and they split John and me up.

I was sent down to Bow where Trollopes were fitting out a huge wood yard shed by the Regents Canal. It was a bit cold and the work was at high level, and I thought sod this and volunteered to make the tea and get the lunches for the team. I managed to string the tidying up of the site hut to the next break each day and that way I stayed in the warm all day while all the mugs did the graft.

Len "The Liar" Morgan was in charge. Len also known as "Captain Morgan" was a bit of a fantasist and we'd keep him talking at tea breaks and lunchtimes to extend them as long as we could. He'd suck on his tobacco pipe, raise his eyes to the ceiling and tell us about all the luxurious cars, expensive artwork, collectable stamps and the enormous yacht he had.

Of course, all his kids were really clever too, unlike us morons.

This from a bloke that lived in a walk-up mansion slum dwelling in Tower Bridge Rd.

The truth was that his kids went to school in Arbour Square, in Stepney. I knew, because Len would pick me up in Commercial Rd on his way to Bow and I'd see him drop them off.

Right, I thought. I won't embarrass him about that, but I'd try to catch him out about his yacht. He was always hard to catch out, though, just like the best of liars.

We were all sat in the site canteen and Len is giving it "The Big I Am" about where he went at the weekend. "I suppose you lot did fuck all at the weekend…Me, I went over to my villa in France with the family in my yacht", says Len, tapping his pipe on his shoe.

"Here, Len…how comes you don't drive your yacht from St Katherine's Dock up the Thames, enter the Regents Canal in Limehouse and sail up to the site every day?"

Everyone goes quiet and turn their heads towards Len.

Len blows his pipe clean…gives it a suck…thinks about it for ten seconds or so and then, with a twinkle in his eye, he says,

"It's got a 10 foot drop keel…it would get stuck in the silly little canal… Right, back to work you lot", and he stood up, winking at me as he walked out. I loved him. He was great entertainment.

There was another apprentice on this site who used to hero worship me a bit. His name was Brett Creswell. Nice kid, but a bit of a loser really. I looked after him though and wouldn't let anyone take advantage of him.

He also bought a scooter just to be like me, only his was an old LD Lambretta. It was something an old bloke would have and no Mod would be seen dead on it.

He turns up for work in Bow with it. He was over 2 hours late and looking out of puff. "Me scooter broke down, I've just pushed it for 5 miles" he says.

"How's your petrol?" I ask. "It was full when I bought it "he replies. So I turn his petrol key over to the standby setting and kicked started it a few times and it starts up.

The poor sod. He thought petrol was like oil. You put it in once a year maybe. He had no idea you had to keep filling it up and, even worse, he had no idea he still had a quarter of a tank left when he started pushing it from Aldgate.

I then moved back to working with "Evil" Sam Milan again who continued to made my life hell, always taking the piss out of me. He'd ask me what religion I was and what football team I supported. Then he didn't stop ridiculing me over both. I thought he was a miserable old git. He had a bald head, black teeth and bad breath, and he still felt he could take the piss out of me.

He was a great sparks, though, and I learned a lot from him, but I hated every minute I spent at work with him and asked to work with another sparks.

We earned extra money from salvaging scrap cable, stripping the insulation off and selling the copper content. Sometimes I'd earn more from scrap copper cable than I did in actual wages.

I remember working with Ian MacDougall (Mac), as his apprentice. I must have been about 18 then. He was a "sweaty sock" (Jock/Scotsman). He was also a rocker (motorcyclist) and another one who thought himself a hard nut, flash bastard, too.

I'd collected a few bags of swag (scrap copper cable) and had sorted out the totty-man (scrap merchant) who gave me £20. I gave Mac his share, which he was delighted with. I shared the money 50-50 with him even though I did all the graft. He later came up to me and gave me a ten bob note (50p) out of the £10 I'd given him. He thought he would be generous and treat me to something. I just waved my ten £1 notes in his face and said "Thanks, Mac. But I've already got my share." He thought he'd be generous and give me 50p out of £10. The tight bastard!

I'd also worked as an apprentice on the temporary lighting (Construction Site Services) side.

These were some of my happiest times at work.

This was where I could earn the extra dosh I needed to keep my scooter going, and to pay for my whistles ("whistle and flutes", suits).

The guys in this division of the firm were much more of a laugh to work with! Great "Graftsmen" and I learned how to bring in the extra loot I needed

I started at "The Stock" (The Stock Exchange Tower) with a fantastic gang of wisecracking blokes

Jim (The Wig) Wiggins who was the foreman,

Vic (Potty) Porter,

Old Jack Welby

Terry (Dopey Doe) Dolan,

Jim (Big Jim) McGilvary

Bill (Fatty) McCarthy

We were supervised by Harry Smith (Smiffy), a lovely man from Highbury who was married a Danish woman. Looking back, Harry was like a second father to me and he did his best to straighten me out.

The temporary lighting job entailed providing the power and lighting to the site workers and keeping all the construction plant going, like the tower cranes, concrete vibrators, hoists and air compressors, etc.

It was exciting and scary and we were the "crème de la crème" on site. The main activity was around "The Slide". This was a huge shutter into which concrete was poured 24/7. The shutter would be jacked up slowly and the result was a concrete core that formed the lift shafts, staircases and riser shafts through the tower. The faster the slide moved, the more bonuses we got; the higher the slide got, the more danger money we got.

We'd be booking 100 hours a week, working "ghosters" (working overnight) and weekends

We were having a problem one day with an electrical pneumatic air compressor and the boys needed a hand. They'd run out of proper 160 amp cartridge fuses. These things were the size of a tea mug and, unknown to me, one of the lads had strung bare wires across the fuse links in the main switch instead of using the proper cartridge fuse. These fuses were full of sand to dampen the explosion of the fuse wire inside them. This occured when there was a massive earth fault.

"Right, switch it on again," shouts one of the lads. So, being helpful and wanting to keep in with them, I volunteered to do it. I stood in front of this huge switch, retracted the long handle from its sleeve and pulled as hard as I could. This was a huge 160 amp, 415 volt switch and fuse assembly, remember.

"BANG"... The whole thing explodes in my face. I stagger out of the temporary switch room with a blackened face and no eyebrows to see all the lads rolling about at my misfortune.

I got over my shock and was now one of the gang. I was officially one of "The Stock".

We seemed to spend most of our time at "The Stock" in a card school, playing Twizzle. A game of luck, skill and bluff. It was a great laugh and you could earn, or in my case lose, a few bob playing it.

Pages from the Daily Express carefully protected the card table; it was a broadsheet newspaper back then. This was carefully folded over the cards if some berk wanting the power put back to the site somewhere interrupted us.

I remember losing all my week's wages in one Friday game, so I was skint for the coming week. I asked the lads if they would lend me the fare home and they just said, "Fuck off.. That'll teach you not to be so stupid", and it worked. I walked home that night with a just packet of chips to eat, totally borasic lint (skint). When I got as far as Aldgate, a tramp approaches me for a chip and I gave him the whole packet.

After working all week, I was no better off than a bum on the street. I didn't gamble heavily ever again in my life. Thanks for that lesson in life, lads.

These blokes were great fun to work with, though. I remember we always went to breakfast at about 10 am each morning. It was a tough and cold job out there on site, especially in winter. We'd all traipse down to Anna's café in Billingsgate fish market and have massive fry ups that kept us going all day. This meant we could play cards all lunchtime too with just a big cup of tea each on the mess table.

Potty Porter had the biggest appetite. He was a big bloke and took some feeding.

"Egg, bacon, sausage, chips, tomatoes, beans and a fried slice, please, Anna darling", he'd shout. I nearly fell off my chair the day he called out "Same again, Anna but with two toast, please!"

The Wig could be described as a good-looking bloke. A bit of a teddy boy. He came from Peckham and was also a bit of a ladies' man. He would only drink shorts, vodka and lemonade, or maybe gin and tonic, where the others would drink pints of beer. Had a lot of style did Jim.

Potty Porter was the clown in the team and he got the lads to teach me another lesson one day. They tied me up with chains and hung me by my feet from the sprinkler pipes on the ceiling and fucked off down the café, giving me a swing for good luck as they all left the lock up.

Jock, the site's banksman, would come in for a game of cards from time to time, and I think it was him and Fatty McCarthy that cut me down after about 20 minutes. They'd have been taken to an employment tribunal nowadays, eh? It just taught me not to be lippy to older people.

Jack Welby was an "electrician's mate". A sparks that had no formal qualifications, but he could do the job. He used to holiday in Leysdown-on-Sea, too, so we had a lot in common.

Big Jim McGilvary was another big guy. He had curly hair, a stutter that we used to tease him about mercilessly and a big chip on his shoulder about bosses. His favourite saying was. "Th-th-they don't f-f-fucking c-c-c-care about me. So why should I f-f-fucking care about them". Big Jim was loved by everyone, but cross him and he'd get you in firm headlock and you were one click from a broken neck!

Dopey Doe was a lovely bloke, too. Short with blonde hair and big blue eyes. He loved a laugh and had a fantastic sense of humour.

Fatty Bill was a good pal to me. He also supported Millwall and took me under his wing.

He and I worked together at the Leadenhall St site (The Lead). It was a big hole in the ground when I first met Billy there. I used to man the site when he was on leave and stuff. I remember coming to site there one Monday morning and couldn't for the life of me understand why no one else was around. I'd been out the night before for afters in a pub and just thought that I'd set my alarm clock wrong and got in too early. So I climbed over the gate and got into our site hut and made me self a cup of tea. I fell asleep in the lock up and work up about 10 am and there was still no one around.

It was a Bank Holiday Monday. What a berk? Billy enjoyed that one.

I could impersonate our foreman, Harry Smith, so well, that I used to phone up the guys and order material or work to be done. I used to love the trouble that would cause.

But the day Harry threw me off The Stock is one I'll never forget. I was turning up too late for work at weekends after a night on the piss and Harry was right to come down on me.

He sent me into the "sin bin", to work on another site with "Evil" Sam Milan's nephew Alan Milan.

I'm telling Alan what happened and I was well into my impersonation of Harry when Alan starts to look a little nervous. I carry on for a few more minutes until I look round and there's Harry, framed by the doorway, right behind me and we stood there looking at each other in exactly the same pose, with exactly the same Trollope and Colls donkey jacket on. I could have died. He was ok about it and just said that I should start doing some work before he fucked me off entirely right back to the boring installation team.

Anyway, a few years later, I "came out of my time" and completed my apprenticeship. I managed to get my hands on some qualifications at long last and was granted the City and Guild's Electricians Certificate and Electrical Installations certificates Part A and B for my college work and was given my apprenticeship indentures. I was now a fully-fledged electrician, just like my old neighbour and inspiration, Phil Coffey, was.

I had managed to get Smiffy to have enough faith in me to give me my own site to look after. Phase 6 of a massive rebuild of the Daily Express building in Fleet St.

Again, it was a big hole in the ground when I first stepped onto the site with the demolition having just been completed and the tower crane base in situ.

The first job was to put the temporary site mains distribution in place and wire up the hoarding lights around the perimeter.

The site started to develop and all the sub contractors had to come to me for their 110v temporary power requirements, to check their plant and for me to connect it up on the site. This plant included welding machines, transformers, compressors, flood lighting, hoists etc.

I was the most sought after bloke on site and I kept everyone sweet!

I'd been there 18 months and I reckoned I was worth a rise as I was now in charge of a site, and so I asked for one. But the new Contracts Manager, Bob Jenkins, told me that this would only happen if I was supervising other electricians. Bob was a likeable bloke, a straight type from the fit out installation side of the firm.

So anyway, I gave it a month and invented a job that I needed help with and asked for Johnny Scott, another young sparks, to come round and help me pull a heavy armoured cable around the site. Johnny turns up and says, "Ok, Dave, what are we doing?" "Don't you know?" I ask humorously.

I rang Bob back and I tell him that there's a bloke turned up on site and doesn't know what to do. "Tell him then" he says. "Oh, you want me to supervise him, right. Do I get the higher rate to do that then, only this job has to be done today otherwise the site stops?" I replied. I got the extra money that day.

We all still meet up on reunions 40 years on and still get on really well. Fatty still calls me "Son" which I like.

Harry sadly died after a debilitating muscle disease hit him. The boys from The Stock and I all went to his funeral. Harry's son, Carl, and his Mum got to hear of my impersonations of Harry and asked me to do it at his wake! They loved it and it put a smile on their faces.

All was going well at work until I had a really bad football injury. It was an innocuous tackle, but it left me lying in agony on the floor while the 21 other players fought each around me.

England football legend, Paul Gascoigne, had the same injury in the famous Spurs Cup Final incident, where he tore his left knee cruciate ligaments and cartilages. It prevented me from playing football again, which really pissed me off as I absolutely lived for it. I was off work for six weeks after the operation to repair the damage.

After my operation, I woke up delirious in a ward in the London Hospital in Whitechapel. It was the same day that our Wapping side, Project One, were playing in a cup semi final over the Hackney Marshes. They were up against a really top side.

The lads came in to see me and, apparently, I told them that "Alan Ball (1966 World Cup legend) was under my bed"! "Alan Ball is under your bed?" they asked. "Is he?" I replied. They all looked at each other and decided to leave me to sleep it off. It was the morphine painkillers making me hallucinate.

I have never experienced pain like it in the days after my op.

When I eventually came home, I was in a full plaster cast from my toes to my groin.

My knee was never the same after that. I made a number of comebacks but had to hang my football boots up. My knee just kept collapsing inwards under me during matches and the pain was awful.

The lads on the Daily Express building site collected £91 for me, which I can tell you was a lot of money in 1972. I recall being amazed by all the names on the letter that came with the money. Most of them were foreign immigrants, just as you would find on building sites today. But, back then, they were mainly Irish labourers and Sikh carpenters. Now, they are all Eastern European lads. I was really touched by that collection and have never forgotten their charity and goodwill to this day.

I acquired some great mates from the London area on that site, too, and we used to go to a local disco pub called The Two Brewers on Friday lunch times and chat up the office girls.

That's where I met Steve Simms. He was a striking looking bloke from East London, almost German looking. We got on like a house on fire and the girls loved the two of us and the fun we used to have. He, too, was an electrician and worked for Rashliegh Phipps Ltd, another contractor on the site. I'd hold the beer money for him and his mates and get the beers lined up for them just before they arrived.

They'd come and go backwards and forwards to the site all afternoon, pretending to be working. As soon as their supervisor had turned his back on the site, it was a case of back to the pub again. Great times. We had a former DJ from Manchester's Piccadilly Radio playing records in the pub. The most popular record at the time was Mr Blue Sky by The

Electric Light Orchestra.

Steve and I would also entertain each other on the tube journey home to the East End each night. He and I would enter the tube train carriage at opposite ends to give the impression we were not with each other. Then he would pretend to be gay and ask me if I was the man he met in some gay club or other and I'd, of course, deny it.

We used to wet ourselves at the reaction of the rest of the travellers in carriage.

I remember chatting up this very attractive girl. Can't remember her name now but she came from South East London. She knew she was a looker too. We were both a bit flash really. We arranged to meet on a date and she never turned up. I was gutted, but the next time I saw her, I pretended I hadn't gone either.

The games you play when you're young and flash eh?

1970
That Benidorm holiday with Danny

*"I thought he was going for a knife and cracked him
another one on the chin to stop him. He then produces a
badge from his pocket. It had "Policia" on it!"*

It was around this time that I first could afford to go on holiday twice in one year. So I asked a good mate, Danny Ferry, if he fancied a week in Benidorm just before Christmas. We'd been there in the summer mob-handed and I wanted a break before the Christmas festivities. So we booked it up.

The Hotel was called the Tres Coronas, which was a good omen as our favourite pub in Wapping was the Three Swedish Crowns anyway.

We got there and, instead of finding ourselves on a coach full of birds from the Alicante airport to Benidorm, we end up in a very small and dodgy looking cab. It stunk of petrol and so would all our holiday clothes for the rest of the trip.

When we got to the hotel we were really up for it. So we came down for dinner (reeking of petrol) only to find the hotel was virtually empty. No matter, we thought, we'll go out and find some birds somewhere. This is Benidorm ,after all.

We toured the streets only to find the whole place shut down for the winter with just one or two security lights in the tall hotels left on. This was a disaster.

We went back to the empty hotel, had a few beers, went to bed early and looked forward to tomorrow.

Nothing had changed the next day and we swam in the pool on our own. Danny was starting to curse me now and I was getting pissed off with his moaning.

The Hotel was advertising a dance that night, so we came down to the bar area alone again (still reeking of petrol) and spent the night listening to what must have been the oldest band in the world. The accordionist couldn't even hold up his own squeeze box. It was on a stand in front of him and he sat down to play it.

When we got back to the room, Danny started moaning again and would not stop. I told him that if he didn't turn it in I'd give him something to moan about. He didn't and I chinned him.

The next day we sat there staring at each other at breakfast with our black eyes and scratched faces and just pissed ourselves laughing at the ridiculous situation we had put ourselves in.

Things improved that night and we found a couple of girls in a bar to go drinking with. We were walking back to our hotel when suddenly a car pulls up alongside Danny and his girl and a fight breaks out. So I storm in to help him as there are two blokes attacking him. I thump one and knock him clean over his car bonnet and he reaches for his pocket. I thought he was going for a knife and crack him another one on the chin to stop him. He then produces a badge from his pocket. It had "Policia" on it! We ran like fuck down a back alley and make it back to the Three Crowns Hotel. A lucky escape.

The next day, we decided to take a boat trip to the Isle of Benidorm, a large rock in the sea off the beach. We found ourselves on a boat with a load of pensioners explaining why we stank of petrol. We decided to lose them and go swimming around the other side of the island. When we came back, the boat had just gone and the next one was in 3 hours time. It couldn't get any worse ,could it? Yes it could and it did.

Danny was well fed up now and staying in his room.

I'm in the hotel bar when a young tour rep comes in looking for a group of people who were going to a Barbeque. So I talk him into letting us join them. I give the guy some cash and go and get Danny from the room. I'd got a bit of a tummy by then but I'm not going to miss this big night out at the top of a mountain.

We go, have a great time and eat and drink plenty. Then it's time to have a dance under the stars before getting into the coach again and returning to the hotel. So I walk onto the dance floor in my white flared trousers and white cheesecloth shirt, feeling a million dollars and get a stomach cramp. I shouldn't have risked it but I farted and shit myself! Not a lot, but enough to send me running to the toilet. I was in there for quite a while and Danny came in chasing me up, as it is now time to go.

When I eventually surface from the toilet, the coach has gone and we were now stranded on the top of a mountain!

The rep had forgotten about the two extras he'd taken on and had left us behind. We had to call for a taxi to come and get us and bring us down from the mountain an hour and a half later. It cost an arm and a leg too.

The holiday from hell was nearly over. It was time to go back to England

and we couldn't wait. The same smelly cab arrived to toke us back to Alicante airport but we were passed caring by then.

We joined the check-in queue and I realised that my airline ticket was missing. I was sure everything would be ok, but, no, they wouldn't let me on unless I could produce a telex showing that I'd paid for a ticket. It was a scheduled flight and not something that could be overcome. It was Sunday and the tour operator's office in Benidorm was closed until Monday.

I was getting hot and bothered now and sat Danny down with my leather jacket and tried to find someone English in the airport who spoke Spanish to get this sorted. But to no avail.

Danny gives me all his spare pesetas and he gets on the plane and I cadge a lift back to Benidorm and check into the Three Crowns again for another night. I hang my suit and shirts up again in the wardrobe. I was hoping to find someone else to lend me some more money so that I could buy a ticket home if I needed to.

There's no one around of course.

I then realise I have left my leather jacket at the airport! So I call the check-in desk in a panic. They can see it and agreed to hold onto it until I come back to the airport the next day.

Meanwhile, on the flight I missed, the airhostess takes pity on Danny and keeps him well fed and watered. Lucky sod!

Later that night, I take a shower and go down to the bar to make the best of it. I meet up with two South American builders who were touring Europe, get talking about my situation and they invite me out to dinner on them. So I think, what the hell, let's have a night out.

I'm on my way back to the room to change, when a female tour courier sitting in reception catches my eye. She is talking perfect Spanish to the receptionist and I enquire how she learned the language.

She tells me she lived in Peru... just like one of the blokes in the bar. So I introduce her to them and the next thing is that we three blokes are going out to dinner with her and her two mates.

We had a fantastic night, dining out in the Hotel Avenida.

I escorted her back to her apartment. We went the long way round so we would avoid bumping into her boyfriend, who was a bouncer and minding the door of a local club. But we couldn't avoid bumping into his mates who gave me a dirty look.

I stayed the night with her in her apartment.

I'm dozing off when I hear an enormous BANG! I leap from the bed and grab my clothes thinking it's the boyfriend and contemplate jumping from the first floor window. Turns out it's just the central heating contactor switching the winter heating on inside a panel on the staircase to her apartment. Phew!

Poor Danny, he missed the best night of the holiday and it didn't cost me a peseta!

The next morning I call the tour operator's office and get the telex sorted which will be sent to the airport later that afternoon.

I'm met by an angry looking old bag of a tour guide who blames me for missing the flight and we argue all the way to Alicante airport.

Guess what? There is no sign of the telex, but I get my leather coat back. I'm really pissed off by then and just want to go home.

The telex finally arrives a few minutes before the check-in closes. I kiss the old bag goodbye, stick my tongue out at the check-in bloke and run to the gate to get plane home.

So all's well that ends well, eh? Not quite I left my suit and shirts hanging up in the hotel wardrobe.

You couldn't make it up, could you?

Stuck on island, stuck at an airport, stuck up a mountain. The blonde courier was a bonus though.

1973
Terror come to the streets of London

*"I virtually ran for my life all the way
to the Tower of London"*

I'm back at work and installing the hoarding lights on a new "hole in the ground" site at WH Smiths in Fetter Lane. There were demolition contractors on the site, blowing up concrete bases with gelignite. It was a safe operation, providing everyone took notice of the warning whistles from the contractor and ducked or hid on hearing the first two and only came out again after the all clear whistle.

I was working on a pair of stepladders with my head above the hoarding and just ducked down at every warning whistle. But then there was an almighty explosion and I was nearly knocked off the ladder entirely.

I gathered myself and climbed the steps again expecting to see a cloud of dust across the open site on the other side of the hoarding, but the explosion hadn't come from the site at all.

Suddenly people where rushing past me in panic, in blood stained clothes, shouting about a bomb or something.

This was all new to us then, so I was interested in finding out more and made my way towards the scene of the incident, just a few streets away. I'd never seen anything like it.

This was the IRA bombing of the Old Bailey. A pub was badly damaged, an office tower block severely wrecked, mountains of glass everywhere and I could see the shell of car burning outside the Old Bailey itself.

Panic set in and I virtually ran for my life all the way to the Tower of London without stopping, and then slowly walked the remainder of the way back home to Wapping.

The City was never quite the same place to work in after that. But it has always been an exciting place to work.

I was working all over the City and the West End and loved it. It was so exciting. I got to hear that the Beatles were about to arrive at the London Pavilion in Piccadilly Circus for the premiere of the cartoon feature film Yellow Submarine. So I stood out there in the rain just to catch a glimpse of them and I did. They arrived in vintage Rolls Royces. Paul was in a black suit and shirt with a lemon kipper tie and looked great and George was in an orange suit and floppy hat.

Then on another occasion, I was lucky enough to see the three U.S. astronauts that went to the Moon.: Michael Collins, who orbited the moon in the spacecraft Columbia, Buzz Aldrin and Neil Armstrong who flew down to Tranquillity Base in the lunar module, "The Eagle".

Neil Armstrong was to become the first man to step foot on the Moon with those famous words "That's one small step for man...one giant leap for Mankind." Here they were right in front of me at the Hilton Hotel in Park Lane. Fantastic.

1970's
Night life in Stepney

"There was a lot of commotion and suddenly a
huge bang and sparks flying across the room.
This was a sawn-off shotgun going off!"

I liked a night out and we used to party big time in the late 60's and early 70's in Stepney.

As I was quite tall at 15 years of age, I was able to convince publicans that I was over 18 and could get into pubs.

We used to get into our local boozers by putting on a deep voice and approach the bar on tip toes and order "A pint of Brown and Mild, mate" and make it last all the night.

We were starting to go to clubs like The White Swan in Commercial Road. They played Ska music in there, which was the earlier form of Reggae. It was music brought over by the West Indian immigrants of the 1950's.

It was a great boozer and we got to know the doormen. It was very dark inside and had multi coloured images of paddleboats and Al Jolson types on the walls. These were painted in luminous paint, and highlighted by ultra violet light fittings, which created a really unusual effect at that time. Any white clothes you wore also really shone out.

It was fairly infamous locally in those days.

We were in there one night at 11pm, when it was raided by a mob of blokes who came in to turn the publican over for his takings. There was a lot of commotion and suddenly a huge bang and sparks flying across the room. This was a sawn-off shotgun going off! We were out of the fire exits like a shot, I can tell you.

Mum's brother, Harry, had offered to get her a job in the Civil Service alogside him, in their duplicating area. She thought this was out of her league as she was still cleaning offices. We talked her into considering it. She took it on and was due to start work at the Foreign and Commonwealth Office in Whitehall, when it suddenly dawned on her that she had never travelled any further than from Wapping to Whitechapel on the tube. So I had to take her to St James's Park and back one Sunday, so that she could learn the route.

Mum took to it well and went through a training programme so that she could work all the various machines. Bless her.

Although she did have a few problems when our great nation decided to change its currency to decimal in 1971!

This was a hilarious time, and many older people just didn't have a clue what was going on. You have to remember that we were not so good at maths anyway, at the time.

Now our £'s, shillings and pence were to be transformed into £'s and new pence as our currency went decimal. We had only just got used to not having farthing coins - there four of them to a penny (1d). The halfpenny coin was also to be phased out. Now we were being told that we would no longer have 240 pennies to a pound, but there would be 100 new pennies instead. We'd no longer have 12 pennies making a shilling and 20 shillings making a pound or have Half Crown coins either. Half-a-crown was 2 Shillings and 6d. The 10-shilling note would also go and would become a 50p coin. There would be no more three-penny bits (3d) or tanners (6d) or florins, which were 2 shilling coins, either.

Just to make it even more complicated for you youngsters, we also called a shilling a "bob", and prices were displayed as 30/6d. This meant 30 shillings and sixpence. Or, to put it another way, £1 and 10 shillings and six pence. This today would be £1.52. Easy innit?

Poor Mum. We used to send her up to Harry Stewart's grocery shop and tell her to buy a loaf of bread and explain what to hand over and what to expect back as change. She'd go into the shop convinced she understood it all and come back totally confused.

Mum was doing well in her new office worker role and we were all so proud of her.

She comes home from work one night in 1973 and is laughing about the fact that they had asked her if she would like to now relocate and work in Brussels at what would become the Common Market Headquarters. We were stunned, but again encouraged her to do it, which she did. What an amazing woman she was. Seems like one minute she's a widow with five kids at school, then a civil servant who doesn't know how to use the London Underground or to use the new currency in her own country, and then she's invited to travel and have her own apartment in the centre of Brussels. She was in the same role in the duplicating area, but now a part of the EEC team.

She would attend functions at the Ambassador's residence too.

We missed her enormously, but she would travel back every month or so, and Barbara, my girl friend at the time, and I went over together to stay with her for a few days in 1973.

We couldn't understand much French and certainly no Flemish at all, and we struggled even to get to Brussels station.

We should have changed trains at one point but failed to do so. We spent the night in a shunting yard, going backwards and forwards as the train picked up more and more carriages for its next trip the following day. We didn't sleep a wink and had no idea what the hell was going on all night.

It rained the whole time we were there, so we went to see the new James Bond film "Live and Let Die". We also had a great meal out with Mum, in what we felt was a very posh restaurant at the time. It was called the Western Steak House, and they brought a tray full of fresh beefsteaks to your table so you could personally select the cut they would then cook right in front of you. All this is now a given in my new lifestyle, but, back then, it was the height of sophistication, and I remember feeling that Mum had come a long way.

With Mum away in Brussels, we now had the run of the home and would hold regular all night parties in no 6 Riverside.

As we got older, we would go to young people's pubs in Stepney, like Kate Hodders, The Carpenters Arms, The Jug House and The Rose and Punchbowl, which had decent DJ's and music in them, and we'd walk from one to the other looking for girls and the girls would do the same.

Just before these pubs would shut, we'd send out a search party to the large pavement area outside the Blind Beggar in Whitechapel. This was the place where anyone who was having an all-night party, or wanted to get invited to one, used to assemble.

You'd be there, lying through your teeth, telling girls you had a party to go to, and could get them into, and telling boys that you hadn't even if you had. Girls came to the parties free but blokes were expected to join in the whip money paying a fiver or a tenner. They would be given the address and told to make their way there.

Once enough money and girls were collected, a few of the blokes had to get to a pub a bit lively and get the drink in. This meant getting wooden crates of beer, and several bottles of Vodka and mixers for the boys, and maybe some Gin and Martini and Babyshams for the girls. If we could get ice, lemons and some glasses, it was a bonus.

The game was to get back quickly to the flat where the party was before the girls shoved off to a better one.

We'd then party until dawn, unless a punch up started.

Then we'd do the same the next week, and the circle of party-going got bigger and bigger and you'd have some bargaining power as you'd invited someone to yours, so they had to repay the compliment.

I had my first real sex after one of these parties when an older woman took a shine to me. She had come to the party with a local pub owner. I'd say she was 40 and I was 17. We were having a smoochy dance when a massive punch up started and we escaped. She invited me back to her luxury flat in Shadwell and taught me all about it.

In the morning, I asked her why she hadn't married. She said she had…. but he was in prison! I was out of there faster than a cat out of hell and stayed as far away as I could from her.

Sleeping with the wife of a villain in prison is something you just don't do in the East End, believe me.

If there was nothing going on in Stepney, we'd go out to Ilford, to the Room at The Top. This was a smashing venue at the top of the Harrison and Gibson store. It could only be accessed by a small 5 person lift from the street and the bouncers would vet every single person going in and turn you away if they didn't like the look of you.

If we were mob handed as blokes, we'd split up and ask girls if we could pretend to be their boyfriends and try to go in as couples. It was a real drag if you couldn't get in, and a long and sometimes lonely trip back to Stepney if one or two of your mates got in and you didn't.

If you did get in you'd be dancing the night away to Barry White's "You're the First, My Last, My Everything", George Macrae's "Rock Your Baby" and "Rock the Boat by The Hue's Corporation.

I met my first real girlfriend around this time. I enjoyed girl's company and would go out with boys all week but I took girls out one on one on Saturday nights.

I first saw Barbara in the Jug House. She was showing off but I was playing it cool. I remember she was in a blue halter neck dress with white polka dots. Freddie Ransome thought he had a chance with her and made a move on her. She brushed him off a bit too quick for his liking and offended him. So he tipped a pint of lager over her head!

I took her under my wing and took her home to no 6. We took my dog Shep for a walk over the bridges and I put my coat around her shoulders when she shivered.

She stayed the night and we were together for 18 months.

The Jug House was a tiny little pub in Stepney Green, but it had a great atmosphere at that time.

When my sister Catherine was marrying her fiancé, Tony North, he held his stag night in there, and it was packed. But there were two separate groups of young men in the pub that night and there was always some friendly rivalry amongst us. We used to bump into this other group on our holidays in Spain, where they would spend the holiday season acting as bouncers on the doors of clubs, or doing some "prop", giving out propaganda notes/invites to young people to stir up trade for a disco or whatever.

It was a great night in the Jug until someone pushed into the bar queue. Dennis Ayris threw a mineral bottle at one of the other blokes and all hell broke loose.

It was just like a brawl in a bar in a Western film. Bottles and stools were being broken across people's heads and it spilled out onto the street and didn't stop for 25 mins at least.

It finally broke up and we all made our way back to Wapping and to our own territory. I felt bad, as I used to play football with the other guys on Saturday as well as with my mates on Sundays. So I knew everyone involved.

A couple of weeks go by and I'm sitting in the Jolly Sailor in Wapping when a large group of young men come in to the other bar. It was the guys from the Jug House. Clearly they felt they had to show their faces in our pub.

The word was out and all the Wapping boys started to fill up the other bar and a staring competition started.

Time for some mediation I thought so I go round to the other bar and have a chat with them. "What are you lot doing round here? 'You lost?" Wapping is well off the beaten track, remember.

"Nah, just thought we'd pop in, like" they said. So we have a drink together and I go back round to the other bar.

They then drank up and left having made their point.

Barbara came to Catherine and Tony's wedding, and Mum, of course, came back from Brussels to be there.

Mum and Barbara got on really well and it was just one of those stupid things that caused us to break up.

I was not ready to get engaged, but all her friends at her workplace were getting married to their blokes within a year of meeting them. So she gave me an ultimatum, and packed me in shortly after we had taken separate holidays in Ibiza.

I'd even taken a bus around the Spanish Island to surprise her, which she loved, but she later met a bloke on that holiday who had given her promises of instant marriage, and she convinced herself that I was wasting her time.

I was just 20 years old, for God's sake, and just finished my apprenticeship. We could have been good for each other, but back me into a corner and you lose, baby! That was how I saw it then anyway.

We parted and she married this bloke in months. It took a long while to get over her. Her family told me years later she'd said she'd made a big mistake.

I was out of my apprenticeship and starting to earn a reasonable living, but, by then, I was getting restless at Trollope and Colls. We'd had a Bicentenary party and I got the last member of the Trollope family alive (Sir Patrick) to autograph the special book they gave us all, which was a nice gesture. But I was in the "sin bin" again and working with a load of tossers on a building site.

My old electrician Chalkie's younger brother, Keith White, was in charge! I thought, no way can I work with him!

Anyway, Keith starts coming the old acid and telling me what to do. At the end of the week, he brings me a time sheet to sign. It has one of the other group member company names on it. He'd docked me a few minutes for being late, the wanker.

So I tell him, "Sorry, I can't sign that, it would be fraud. I work for Trollope and Colls, mate". He was livid, but I didn't care.

I rang Ernie Goldsmith at Trollopes and told him that I wasn't happy working for another firm in the group. He said it would be ok to sign the timesheet, as we are all one firm now. I told him that if Trollopes had no work for me they should make me redundant and then I'd choose who I worked for. Now Ernie was livid too. They found me a Trollope's site with another load of tossers.

Then something really significant in my working life happened.

I was about to resign from Trollope's and move on when I saw an advert saying "Refrigeration Engineers Required, Mortimer Gall Ltd".

Mortimer's was a company that Trollopes had taken over, as part of the mergers with Trafalgar House Group, and here's me asking to work for one of them now.

I was a real handful at the time.

I applied for the job in the hope that they would train me for it and they agreed to take a chance on me. It could keep me out of trouble, they thought.

This took me into the third string of the firm I mentioned earlier and I loved it. It was a complete change from site work and I soon had my own van travelling the South East of England, installing and maintaining air conditioning units. These were mostly in branches of Barclay Bank. This meant I could chat up the girls in the banks, who liked a bit of rough like me and saw me as a big change from the office wallies around them.

It was during my time with the air conditioning team that I met Johnny Brown (Brownie). He was the closest I got to a real pal on the firm at that time as I didn't see the boys from The Stock any more.

We had exactly the same sense of humour. We'd meet in the yard on Mondays to be issued with our Barclays job cards for the next fortnight or so. I'd spot his van and I'd put a parking ticket I'd received onto his windscreen to frighten the shit out him.

He'd retaliate weeks later by loosening/bending my windscreen wipers or wing mirrors. It got out of hand when we started letting each other's tyres down or taking each other's bloody wheels off though. I'd love to see him again.

I managed to find another way of increasing my income too. I was parking up in the City one Monday and I could see someone up to no good at the parking meter next to me. This was in the days when you would put a shilling in for say 30 minutes' parking.

So I ask him what he's up too and he lets me in on his scam.

He'd recognised that the meters were clockwork and that the meter maids only wound them up once a week. He had developed a technique to unwind them. The trick was to put the shilling halfway in and pull it out and watch the meter wind on. You repeated this procedure rapidly over the next 15 mins until there was no more energy in the clock work system and then put your shilling in. The meter would not wind on and register any penalty flags for the meter maids to spot.

This was great and I made sure that I was always parked in the same bay all week for free and just booked the £15 parking as an expense each week. You have to be creative in this world and try to beat the system where you can eh?

I was playing records in the Three Swedish Crowns pub (Bullens) in Wapping now and the van would come in handy for ferrying the records around in.

Billy Jones owned the pub and me and all the lads from Wapping used to frequent it 7 nights a week. It was probably the best time of our lives.

We were young and carefree and the pub was really, really lively. We'd have Home and Away pool matches in the week, a live band would play Friday and Saturday nights, and I'd play records there on Thursday and Sunday nights. We'd come back there after we'd played football over Hackney Marshes on Sunday mornings before going home for Sunday dinner with Mum and then be back again at 8:30pm to do it all again.

Bill had his favourites and, once we got rid of the mug punters who only used to spend a couple of quid, he'd lock the doors, have a whip round and we'd have "afters" (drinks after the legal closing time) all night. Sometimes he'd go to bed and leave us to pay up and lock up. Public houses had to close at 2pm on Sunday afternoons and at 11pm on any other night. That was no good to us as we were just getting the flavour by then.

We used to get "the old bill" knock on the door at times, but we'd ask them in and tell them how much we appreciated them and give them a few drinks too. No problem, sorted.

We had fancy dress nights too, which were great fun. But, one night, a nasty fight broke out that was just ridiculous. You had Superman fighting Batman and Robin, and a Vicar and a Nun with their hands around each other's throats!

My air conditioning job had given me many additional skills. So I was becoming popular with the local publicans, as I could finish early at the banks and maintain a few beer coolers and cold shelves in the pubs for a few quid on the side.

I was aware that I was developing skills and getting more income than some of my Wapping mates who had been more successful than me at school. Many of them had married young and had children, so there was signs of envy creeping in at my carefree lifestyle.

I was getting fed up driving the air conditioning van all day and all night, and spotted a nice little car and bought it.

It was a royal blue Triumph Spitfire convertible sports car and I loved it.

1975
David Sapsford and his life-changing accident

*"He caused a stir at the hotel pool after he dived in
and his prosthetic marble eye popped out."*

It was also around this time that one of my Wapping mates, David Sapsford, had the most awful car accident. He'd fallen asleep while driving over Canning Town flyover and he was thrown through the windscreen when the car went out of control and crashed.

David lost the sight in one eye and most of the sight in the other. His face was severely damaged too. We all came together to support him as best we could.

He, Rob and I would still go and watch Millwall, but we'd have to give him a commentary on what was happening if the game crossed the half way line and away from the Cold Blow Lane end of the Den.

At one game though, he nearly got himself into some bovver. It was Millwall v Chelsea and the fans did not like each other one bit.

Rob and I are standing in our usual place just above the players tunnel on the Cold Blow Lane end, when, just before kick-off, Chelsea's hooligan element break the gates down and charge onto our terraces.

We are all forced onto the pitch and the police move us onto the East terrace, leaving the Chelsea lot on what is traditionally the Millwall home fans' end.

We are not happy.

Anyway, Davey arrives late and positions himself where he would expect to find us. Rob and I can see him looking for us amid all the away fans. The trouble is he does not know this. They all have blue football scarves and bobble hats. Both teams play in royal blue.

The Chelsea fans start up a familiar clapping routine that Millwall also use. The fans raise their arms in the air clap in rhythm and then shout the name of their team.

It would go something like;

Clap clap... clap clap clap clap... clap clap clap clap MILLWALL !

Dave joins in thinking he's amongst his own crowd and shouts MILLWALL just as the rest of them shout CHELSEA. He suddenly realises he is in deep trouble and legs to the East terrace and safety before he is beaten to death by the Chelsea shed-end boys.

Millwall actually got quite good in the 70's, when Keith Weller and Derek Possee joined the Lions from Spurs and we nearly got promoted to the top flight. But Leyton Orient let us down by drawing their last game as Brisbane Rd. Birmingham City went up instead.

The family was extending now and I really took to being an uncle. I loved spending time with Pat's boys, David and Paul. When they were old enough I took them with me to watch Millwall. They loved it and would stand either side of me under my long overcoat in the rain, clad in their Millwall hats, scarves and rings.

I can still remember my nephew David turning to me at one home game in the 70's and, after listening to the crowd chanting, he says, "Uncle David, who's going to get their fucking head kicked in?"

They were with Rob and me on the appalling night of violence at Luton when the Millwall hooligans tore the ground apart and fought pitched battles with the local constabulary.

"No one likes us, no one likes us
We are Millwall, we are Millwall
We are Millwall, from the Den".

I stopped taking them after that for many years.

Davey Sapsford was determined to make the most of life after his terrible injury and he did. We talked him into coming away on a holiday to Spain with us in the months after his accident.

Rob was not keen on flying any more so he, Dave and I booked onto a train to meet up with rest of the Wapping boys in Spain.

We were hoping to share bunks on the train with some birds but were lumbered with two old dears and an even older bloke. They didn't like the look of us either, but we won them over with our East End charm.

It turns out that the old boy only has one eye too, so we got them to change seats so that Dave and he could both see out of the window without craning their necks too much. We did laugh about that.

In the next carriage were three or four tossers from Northampton who were going on holiday abroad for the first time. We taught them how to play Twizzle and won most of their spending off them.

They had a song they had made up so they could pull girls with it...it went.

"We're from Northampton Town so get your knickers down".

We stayed in the same resort as them and every time we heard them coming along singing this bloody song we'd hide until they passed by.

Dave was really coming out of his shell now. Girls would ask about his horrific facial injuries and he'd tell them that he was blown up defusing an IRA bomb in the City and he'd get all the girls.

He caused a stir at the hotel pool after he dived in and his prosthetic marble eye popped out. We cleared everyone out of the pool and searched the bottom of it until we recovered it and a big cheer went up poolside.

After that one of us would keep it in a pocket if he went in the pool or the sea.

He'd play tricks on us by popping this marble eyeball into our drinks when we weren't looking. This first time you'd spot it was when you'd finished your drink and there it was, nestling in the ice and lemon at the bottom!

We all went on a summer holiday to Tunisia. It was one of the last times we all did this together as young men. It was just after the entertainer Bruce Forsyth had holidayed there in the same hotel in Hammamet over the previous winter

We become friendly with the bar waiters Ahmed and Mohammed and I was exchanging stories about how tough their lives in Tunisia were compared to ours in London. We were discussing health service provision and "Davey one-eye" is sitting quietly next to me reading a James Bond book.

I explained that David had had "cosmetique" surgery and had a false eye provided by the NHS. Dave taps his marble eye with his beer glass and the waiters shrink back from the table aghast.

He takes it out and offers it to them in the palm of his hand and they call all the others waiters to our poolside table.

"Shufti, Shufti" they shout, beckoning the other waiters to our table.

After much Arabic conversation, Ahmed asks David..."and you see with this?" Well, we nearly fell off our stools laughing.

Thankfully Dave's original swollen scars have subsided over the years and he later married his new girlfriend, Carol, and they and their children now live happily in Blackheath in South London.

1978
Mum dies

"I suffered physically for weeks after Mum passed. I'd awake in the night with massive, violent, crushing pains in my chest. It was as if I was having a heart attack. My doctor just said it was normal and gave me nothing for it. "Anxiety" he said. Undying love and heartache, I'd call it."

Mum came back from Brussels having completed 3 years of duty in the EEC building out there. She'd done really well and we were so proud of her.

My Mum was an incredibly lovely woman. I have a particular fond memory of her.

She used to sing a song to me while she rocked me as a baby/toddler (and perhaps the other boys). I can actually remember her doing it. The song was recorded by Vera Lynn and went "My Son, My Son, you're everything to me. My Son, My Son, you're all I'd hoped you'd be." She, like her own stepmother, brought up 5 kids with little or no support at all from Dad's family.

I loved her dearly.

She died suddenly in 22nd May 1978, in the same flat (6 Riverside) as Dad did. Thirty years later, I still miss her terribly. My sister Pat told me recently I was Mum's favourite, but I never knew that at the time. Mum was a gentle soul and deserved better. She, like Dad, would die before reaching retirement age.

The last time I saw my Darling Mum alive was the 21st May that year. She was on her way up to bed and turned and said "What time do you want a call in the morning, son?" Yes.... I was 27 years old and Mum was still making sure I got up in the mornings after a night on the piss. I can't remember my actual reply, but I would have been due up about 7am, I reckon.

I was woken earlier than that.

My brother Rob was standing at the bottom of my bed stuttering..."It's Mummy.... I er... I think she's er.... wossiname... yer know....she's....".

"Oh fuck me… No Rob!... Mummy!… "I shouted out, leaping from bed and running into her room. Rob later told me this was the second time he'd tried to rouse her that morning. I didn't know that at the time and went straight into life saving mode. I had training as a first-aider and, if anyone could save her, I could.

Mum was still warm but that was because she was wrapped up warm and cosy in bed.

I checked her mouth for her false teeth and started mouth-to-mouth straightaway. I knew I was doing it correctly as I can still remember her lips sort of blubbering back at me after each breathe I put into her.

"Call an ambulance, Rob…" I shouted. "Yeah…..but…", he says. "Rob, just fucking do it…. please". "Then ring Pat and tell her to come over, mate". Pat lived within a half a mile of us, just across The Highway, in Shadwell.

Rob was trying to tell me that she'd been like this for hours and that I was wasting my time. But I didn't want to hear that. I was going to give her the best chance I could anyway.

The Ambulance came and I showed the guys what I had been doing. They asked Rob how long she had been like this and that's when I first knew it was the end.

"Are you sure, mate…have you seen someone like this before? Please, she's still warm…" I pleaded

"It's all over, mate," he said. I almost collapsed in grief. But kept it under control and went downstairs to stand at the kitchen sink. I poured some water over my face.

How could I tell Pat? We'd all be in great shock but, with two very young boys (David and Paul), she saw Mum more than any of us.

The ambulance men were about to take Mum away to the London Hospital (they can't pronounce death, only a doctor can) when Pat burst in.

"What's happened…" she cried. "Where's Mum?"

She knew what I was going to say. I just echoed what the ambulance man said to me. "It's all over, Pat….. She's gone…."

Pat then let out this awful, howling scream as if she was going to be sick, and I led her into the front room while the ambulance lads did what they had to do. To this day, I wished I'd let Pat spend some more time with Mum instead of her having to see her the next time in her coffin.

Over the next few days, my brother-in-law, Bobby, came with me to get the death certificate and order a coffin with funeral director, Alf Tadman; and he was a great help to me.

The manager at the funeral parlour was showing me brochures of his coffins. "This one is our Galaxy range sir...this one is from the standard range". It was just like buying a car really and he had the most awful voice to go with it.

I asked him if he could actually show me one or two so I could pick the best one and do Mum justice without spending a ridiculous sum. Bobby looked a bit sheepish at this point.

We were taken through to the workshop and I saw a coffin on a set of trestles, which I liked. The guy then starts to take the top off. At this point Bobby legs it out the door as he thought there might be a stiff inside it!

It was a very sad time. But I did laugh at that incident much later and have reminded Bobby of that day ever since.

A couple days after Mum died, I phoned in and told my manager that I would be off work for a week.

Mum came home from the parlour and was laid out in exactly the same place in the front room as Dad was. It was strange but I could only sleep again once she was back at home. As the date of the funeral approached, I didn't want to let her go. All my friends came and paid their respects to her, which I appreciated. Her brother, Wilf, could not go in to see her, though, and he just stayed in the kitchen. None of Dad's family came, as I recall.

I was really pissed off that the undertaker did not manage to capture her lovely smile, so I kept her mouth covered with a veil while she was lying in her open coffin in the front room. On the day of the funeral, Rob and I wore the same clothes as twins again. Mum would have liked that.

We held a wake afterwards in the flat, but Rob and I needed to be with our mates. So we all went off to the Three Swedish Crowns where we knew they would be. I broke the ice by putting some cash into a pint glass and we all got pretty pissed that night. The band was playing in the pub and we made it clear that we wanted everyone to have a good drink with us.

Later in the evening, Derek Lawler, one of our mates and a very good singer, climbed on to the stage and said he wanted to sing something for us. He sang Simon and Garfunkel's "Bridge over Troubled Water". It really touched me then and it still affects me now whenever I hear that song.

I suffered physically for weeks after Mum passed. I'd awake in the night with massive, violent, crushing pains in my chest. It was as if I was having a heart attack. My doctor just said it was normal and gave me nothing for it. "Anxiety" he said. Undying love and heartache, I'd call it.

When I did go back to work a week later, I told my manager face to face that I would have to take some more time off to sort out stuff late in the afternoons. I did not really care if I ever worked again at the time, but thought I should try to get some work done for the good of the firm. The manager says, "Well, how long is this going to go on for?"

I was stunned. He had no idea how I was feeling at all. "How long?" I says… "How long…? As long as it fucking takes, alright, you dickhead?" He backed off, but I knew my response would come back to haunt me one day. Mum did everything for us and I did not know where to start without her.

I was going out a pretty blonde from East Ham called Denise Murphy at the time. I quite fancied her and she was really looking forward to her holiday when Mum died so suddenly.

I decided not to tell Denise that week but let her go away without knowing at all.

I couldn't wait for her to come back and went to see her at her home and sobbed about the week I'd had, burying Mum while she was away.

She said she couldn't handle it and virtually showed me the door. I was broken hearted again by another shallow Essex blonde.

There's a lesson here, guys. Don't let any girl you fancy go on holiday abroad, right!

My life was at a crossroads and things could only get better from now on.

1978
I meet Mrs. Right

*"If only the two of them could have met. Maria would
then have had a better insight into why I still cry so
much over losing my darling Mum."*

It was while I was working in a branch of Barclays Bank as an air
conditioning engineer that I met Maria, the girl who was to become my
wife. She caught my eye straight away and I was onto her with my best
chat up line!

I had to climb over her desk to get out onto the roof to install some pipe
work. "Hello" says I. "Dave's the name, sex is me game, what can I do for
you?" She just blushed and said, "Go away with you", or something. Turns
out she's courting a big long streak of piss named Frank. I used to see
them meeting up at lunchtime and later tease her about him.

I was sure we could make a good couple long term, even then.

I went back a few months later to finally commission the air conditioners
I'd installed. I tried to get out of the job because I was embarrassed she'd
given me the elbow when I asked her out.

I walked in and she ran out to the loo. I thought, bugger this, and I did
a quick once over on the air conditioners before she came back into the
office. The unit was full of rubber bands for some reason.

I didn't know at the time but Maria and her friend had been firing
rubber bands into the unit to make it fail so I would come back to repair
it. The day I arrived she found herself with no makeup on and had run off
to make herself up for me.

By the time she'd finished I'd gone, because I felt she couldn't stand to
be in the same room as me.

About six months later, I was sent to another branch of Barclays in
Finsbury Park, North London.

As I arrived, I spotted Maria behind the counter and thought "Oh No,
it's that bird again".

This time she was different, though, and asked me straight and made
me a cup of tea with biscuits. So I ask her "Are you still going out with that
big long streak piss?" "No", she says.

"Wanna go out then?", I ask. "Yeah, alright then", she says.

I took her to the best pubs in the East End, which she liked. We'd see comedians like Jim Davidson, Michael Barrymore, Jimmy Jones, Mike Reid and I'd drive her home to Enfield where she lived. I'd drive 44 miles a night, picking her up and dropping her off again and getting myself home again. She was worth it and I thought, "I'm going to marry this girl someday".

I remember one night in particular. We were being entertained by comedian Roger de Courcey and Nookie Bear in a Pub in Hackney. Maria was getting worried about the bear picking on people and she pulled round to the other side of the stage. I had to remind Maria that this was a ventriloquist act and we had better get back to the side where the dummy was!

Everything seemed to be going well. But Maria went off on a previously arranged holiday to Malta with her friend Liz and, when she came back, she packed me in for a Maltese boy she'd met while she was away.

Oh well, I thought, here we go again. Her loss.

I was getting pretty good as a DJ now and drawing quite a following. People used to ask me to provide the music at their weddings, but I only had a 2nd hand deck that I used to plug into the pub's amplifier and speakers and some old records.

Another publican also asked me to DJ at his pub. It was called "The Londoner", at Limehouse, and it had a late supper licence. This meant that pubs could sell drinks until 2am if they were accompanied with food.

So some pubs would sell chicken in a basket with chips and you could drink the night away until 2am. Most people weren't bothered about the food really.

So I decided to take the DJ thing seriously and invested in a completely new system and became the resident DJ in Virgo's discothèque and I loved it.

The place was banged out every Friday night and I was the man!

This was around 1977 and the music scene was now dominated by the Bee Gees and John Travolta after Saturday Night Fever and Grease hit the cinemas.

Sounds corny now but I'd hold elimination dance competitions and the prize was a bottle of champagne for the best John Travolta and the best Olivia Newton John. The couple left on the floor would not know each other at the start but probably got off with each other later that night.

Fabulous times. I was booked up for 18 months ahead at any one time.

This meant I had to miss most of my friends' parties, weddings, etc, that I was getting invited to. But I was getting anything from £150- £250 a night to play records at weddings and having a great time. If I was lucky enough that the wedding hall closed at 11pm, I'd get back to the East End and have a few beers in a club myself before it closed a 2am.

So, anyway, I'm working hard, earning well and DJ-ing at Virgo's, when a familiar face approaches the stage at midnight. It's one of the girls from one of the branches of Barclays Bank. "You'll never guess who's over there with us. Maria Kelly!" she says.

I acted dumb, but I was really pleased. Maria came to the stage and asked to come up, but I told her that she'd cramp my style with the other girls in the club! I didn't know at this time that she had brought her friends to the club without telling them she knew I worked there. She'd finished with the bloke she met on holiday and realised we were good together, just as I had thought we were.

We agreed to give it another go and, again, the rest is history and we are still together over 27 years later.

Maria Kelly was the best thing to happen to me. She was great fun and wanted the same things I did from life.

I kept my social life with the Wapping lads and with her separate, and gave her my best attention. I wanted to marry this girl.

Maria was still working in Barclays at Finsbury Park close to the Arsenal ground. The club had their account at the branch and she knew all the team. The club asked her to be the hostess when Arsenal opened the first ever Executive Club at a football ground.

Arsenal won the F.A. Cup 1979 and I got to hold the FA Cup myself. I had a maintenance visit to do at the branch but held it off as long as I could.

It had been agreed that if Arsenal were to win the Cup it would come to the branch on the following Monday. Thanks to a great goal by Alan Sunderland it did and I drove up to the branch and the Bank Manager showed me into his office and let me pick it up and raise it above my head. Fantastic or what?

Mum was still alive when I first met Maria but died while we were not seeing each other and they never met. If only the two of them could have met. Maria would then have had a better insight into why I still cry so much over losing my darling Mum.

1980
Time to move on

"Riverside was subsequently renovated and each flat was sold for approx £250,000 each and they are still highly desirable now."

Rob and I were being offered a lump sum to move from No 6 Riverside and stuck out for a decent settlement from the council.

They wanted to demolish Riverside, and any remaining good neighbours were taking alternative homes in the new houses being built on the Dock Basins in Wapping.

This was going to be a real wrench for us both. We'd lived in these flats for 30 years and our parents both died in no 6. But life was changing and we didn't want to be left out of the new homes that were being built. Riverside was not what it used to be and neither were Rob and I

We were now living amongst people who didn't give a shit about how they lived or how it affected anyone else. The caretakers had long gone I suspect we were one of few residents who were actually still paying rent. The rest were on the "Rock and Roll (the dole, social welfare). I managed to get Rob and me a brand new single bedroom council flat each and £1,000 disturbance allowance.

It turns out the council did not pull down our Riverside Mansions home at all. For a few years, students from a local University occupied them. Rob liked that as he used to go to the parties they'd have. Riverside was subsequently renovated and each flat was sold for approx £250,000 each and they are still highly desirable now.

Anyway, Maria and I went out on a shopping spree to buy furniture for my flat. Furniture we could use, maybe, in our first home when we later get married.

We went to the store with a mate of hers and, while I was busy picking out tables and chairs, a telly and a cooker, I turns around and find Maria and her mate winking and giving the thumbs up to each other. They were really enjoying it and so was I, really.

I'd worked hard, earned and saved a few quid and could buy new stuff, so what the hell.

Things were looking up for me, but I was worried that Rob was not coping so well on his own in the flat next door. I was feeling guilty about my future happiness with Maria. I was one half of a pair of twins and wanted us both to be happy.

I still had the family dog, Shep. He was getting older now and was living with me in the new flat. The poor sod's health had deteriorated.

I took the painful decision to take him to the vet and have him put to sleep. It was one of the most awful things to do. Shep made it even tougher on me by leaping into the back seat of my car for the first time ever. The vet gave him a pre-med and I sat on the floor with him crying my eyes out as he drifted off. The vet called me after about 10 mins to seal his fate while I held him.

I came back home to his empty basket, wept again and rang Maria to tell her I had just killed my best friend. She was a great comfort.

We were becoming a real couple and things were really starting to look up for me again.

But around this time Trollopes were struggling on the air conditioning side. So, as I could do both refrigeration and electrical work, I was moved back to being an electrician to save an engineer being made redundant. I'm sure this was all down to that manager who upset me when Mum died. This was no good to me as I was keen to develop more skills and did not want to go backwards.

An old mate from the temporary lighting side told me about a small firm in Camden that were looking for a young Assistant Manager. I met the guy I'd be working with in The Blind Beggar and we hit it off. So I jacked in Trollopes after 13 great years and joined H.E. Carrols.

I was told I was being silly to leave and should hang on until I got my redundancy. This would be something I would hear every time I moved jobs. I was keen to see how far my increased skills could take me. Hanging around until someone told me I was not required was never on my agenda.

But I have to admit this particular move was a mistake from the start.

Our first management task was to sack 6 electricians for "knocking off early". That means going home and booking a full day to you. Then we went onto a Tape Factory where a new installation that had just been completed had taken out the electrical supply to the whole factory.

Their standard of work and the people they employed were a long way behind Trollope and Colls' standards and I was starting to think I should never have left Trollopes.

The guy who'd taken me on decided to jack it all in (leave without notice) a week after I joined him and I handed my notice in a month later.

It was the rewiring of a block of flats in Camden that was the final straw. The electricians under my control were expected to work inside occupied premises and the people living in them were the lowest of the low.

One sparks refused to work in one place because there was a drunken bloke sleeping in the bedroom he was supposed to be drilling holes through. I just pulled the bed over to one side and told him to carry on.

The next guy to stop work told he wouldn't work in "Cat Woman's" house. I went up to see her with him. She had fifteen cats in her flat and they were pissing and shitting everywhere.

I couldn't blame him.

It got to the point where I felt I'd rather be unemployed than work for this lot. So I gave them a week's notice and I was then out of work for a week before I had a stroke of good luck.

Jimmy Flint, one of my Wapping mates, had continued boxing after we all finished, and he had then turned pro and was doing really well under Terry Lawless at the Royal Oak gym in Canning Town.

I used to watch him train and would help him and his (soon to be World Champion) stablemates, Frank Bruno, Maurice Hope, John Stracey, Lloyd Honeygan, by holding their feet down while they did sit ups and stuff. I really missed being a boxer and loved being in and around the gyms and boxers again.

We'd all go and watch Jimmy box at the Albert Hall and Wembley where he had 24 of his 30 fights. Jimmy won 27 of those fights, 17 by knock out. He was a real banger and the press called him "The Wapping Assassin".

Coach loads of us would go from Bill's pub. We'd have a whip round, take our own booze into the box and have a feast of seafood and bagels, watch the fights and then return to the pub for "afters", even more drinks behind closed doors. The pubs still officially closed at 11pm and we'd be in there until 2:30am, sometimes later.

Jimmy won the Southern Area Featherweight title by beating Mark Bliss at the Royal Albert Hall in May 1977, but he never really reached his full potential. He lost his only British Title fight to Pat Cowdell in Feb 1980 and retired a year later when he was KO'd by Steve Sims in an eliminator to fight Cowdell again. Jimmy has never really got over those loses to this day.

I was dropping Jimmy off at one of his training sessions a week after leaving Carrolls when I spotted a Job Centre sign in a market square in

Canning Town. I made some enquires, arranged an interview and got a new job with the BBC as a shift maintenance engineer.

Funny how these things happen, isn't it?

This photograph, taken around 1954, shows Sister Teresa (she was lovely), in a typical scene, looking after the infants in St Patricks R.C. nursery in Wapping

This is the only photograph of my family all together as one group. A treasured memory.

We were on summer holiday in Essex. This photo was taken in the Brooklands Social Club at Jaywick Sands Holiday Camp around 1960.

From top row L-R: My elder brother Johnny, twin brother Robert, elder sister Pat.

Seated L-R: Me, Mum Kathleen, younger sister Catherine and Dad John.

Out on the town. This was taken around 1969, in Wapping, outside The Prospect of Whitby, the oldest Inn on the River Thames.

Left to right: Patrick Fleming, Charlie Ruskin, Me (striking a pose), Robert Exley, and Dennis Cochlin

Our first holiday to Spain. From left to right Dennis Cochlin, Robert Exley, Charlie Ruskin and me. 10 days full board for £25 and 1 shilling. Yes, I am drinking crème de menthe !

This is me and the Wapping boys resting during a kick-around on the red ash football pitch in Wapping Park.

From left to right. Me, Terry Massett, Jimmy Flint, Tony Ransome (hidden), Danny Ferry, my twin Robert (arms raised) and Freddie Burns. That's Graham Burgess popping out through the gate for a comfort break

Project One FC on Hackney Marshes, one of a number of East End football teams I'd played for before injury sidelined me in 1978. We were one big, happy family in more ways than one.

From L-R top row: Me, Tony Thomas, his brother Stephen Thomas, my twin brother Robert Exley, Johnny Wood, Alan Bentley, his brother Wally Bentley, Alan Platt and my elder brother Johnny Exley

Bottom row L-R: Davey Jones, Alan Moore, his brother Freddie Moore, Danny Ferry and Dennis Ayris.

Mickey Gittleson (left) joins me to celebrate Jimmy Flint (centre) winning the Southern Area title at the Royal Albert Hall on 31/5/1977.

My Broad St ABC dinner show at Canary Wharf, November 24 2008.

Top left: Johnny Gleed, Club Trainer of over 40 years, 3rd left Me, 5th left "The Wapping Assassin", former Southern Area Champion Jimmy Flint, 6th left "TV Contender Winner" Michael Lomax. Bottom right: Reigning WBC Champion Nicky Cook.

My Trollope and Colls Electrical Ltd reunion 2008. 42 years on, we still get on like a house on fire, but it's getting harder to tell the sparks from their apprentices these days.

Top row from L-R: Alan Golding, Alan Bourne, Driver Terry Trievnor, Jim (The Wig) Wiggins, John Parry, Jim (Wally) McGilvary, Dave Tull, Gary Blewitt, Steve Edwards

Bottom row from L-R: Bob Jenkins, Bob Bayles, (Fatty) Bill McCarthy, Me, Terry Quinlan , Eric Galloway, Reg Tull.

Clifford Chance's visit to our service provider's office in Mumbai, India.

Seated from left to right: Project Manager Claire O'Brien, Regional Chief Operating Officer Amanda Burton, Me and our (aptly named) Finance Director Stephen Purse.

*That's it ! My 10th (and last) London Marathon in 2005. I have raised
over £30,000 for the Cancer Macmillan nurses. This last race was
dedicated to my old friend Billy Jones, the guv'nor of The Three Swedish
Crowns in Wapping, who had died the previous year.*

This photo, taken in 1987, looking East over Canary Wharf, shows just how the docklands landscape changed in my lifetime.

The Docklands Light Railway line now spans the original dock basins ahead of the new office development to come. The Thames Barrier is in place, but no sign yet of the O2 arena, formerly known as the Millennium Dome, of course.

The change at Canary Wharf over the 22 years is quite remarkable. I'm not sure what my old Dad, a former London docker, would have made of it of it all.

© Canary Wharf Group

*The Old meets the New. Here I am in Shadwell Basin in 2008 just yards
from where I used to stand in the 1950's and watch my Dad John at work in
Brussels Wharf. Now the docks stand idle and Canary Wharf has became my
place of work instead.*

© *Siobhán Doran Photography* **www.siobhandoran.com**

1980–1986
The BBC years

"Call security quick, mate; let's get some help fast",
I reply. But just as he grabs my radio handset to do so,
I pull out the headless body from the cubicle."

I started work with "Auntie" in 1980 at the World Service radio station in Bush House, in London's West End. The World Service was set up during the 2nd World War to broadcast around the world. It still provides news in their native tongue to 250 million people to this day and many still cling to transistors radios around the world trying to understand what is going on in their own countries.

I'd spend 6 happy years with the Beeb and enjoy it immensely. There were some real characters in the maintenance team.

Manager Andrew Galloway, who I liked and admired very much, led us. He was posh and well educated, and I quickly had an impersonation of him off to a tee.

I was nearly caught out doing one at the breakfast table one day as Andrew crept up beside me and lent into the conversation we were all having. One of the engineers, Peter Singfield, was egging me on, as he could see Andrew approaching the table over my shoulder. I forgave him for trying to drop me in it and we are still great friends today.

We were supervised by George "The Greek" Peristiani. He liked a drink and he and I got on well. There were a couple of straight guys, Keith Thornton and Mike Barnes, and two plant attendants, George Spencer and Frank Viegas who came from Goa. George had a part time job as a butcher and would grow vegetables in a skylight on the roof (plant attending!) and Frank would brew and then sell potcheen to the BBC newsroom boys. Apparently everyone does this in Goa.

George the Greek and I got on well with the landlord's House Manager and he would open the bar up again after midnight so we could have a quiet drink before crashing out in an armchair somewhere for the later stages of the night shift.

A Liverpudlian 'deaf and dumber' (plumber), Terry Turner, completed the shift. Terry was a typical working class lad from Liverpool, loved to tell jokes and thought the world owed him a living. He was a bit of a scally, as they say from that part of the world.

He was always pulling my leg. But I caught him out big time one day. It was the weekend and the studios were relatively quiet. I'd recently completed a first aid course and Terry had been teasing me about it. He thought it was something only boy scouts would do.

Anyway he is showering ready to make his exit from the building and I had the wicked idea of faking someone's death in the toilets adjacent to the showers.

I very quickly grab a boiler suit and some wellies, stuff them full of newspapers, etc, to make a body shape, position "the body" in a toilet cubicle and close the door slightly.

I then wait around the corner with my first aid bag over my shoulder and my radio handset in my hand. Terry is blithely unaware and singing Beatles songs at the top of his voice in the changing room.

The door from them opens and I come running around the corner in pretend panic.

"What's up, Dave?" says Tel. "I knew it, it's you innit? Winding me up again", I reply.

"I dunno what you're talking about, I ain't done nuffin," he says.

So I explain that I've had a call from Security for a first aider to attend the changing rooms because someone has been reported to have had a heart attack!

"It wasn't me, Dave, honest, mate; we'd better check it out". He says getting anxious.

"Right, you check the toilet cubicles and I'll check out the showers", I order, going into professional first responder mode.

Terry starts kicking doors open and I know any minute now he'll get to the one with "the body" in. I can't contain myself. He kicks the last door and it doesn't open fully as it hits my patients leg. "Heyup, Dave, mate, He's in here. Fuck me, mate, he's out cold on the floor. What should I do?" he shouts.

"Call security quick, mate, let's get some help fast", I reply. But just as he grabs my radio handset to do so, I pull out the headless body from the cubicle. There's a moment of silence as the penny drops and then we burst into laughter. What a riot. He knew who the daddy was after that.

We had another great laugh one day when he and I decided to play a trick on the staff at the Beeb. We were working on some plant on the roof of Bush House. It overlooked the car park in the centre of the building.

We had a fake £5 note and I glued it to the floor of the car park and watched as we worked. One of the radio presenters spots it as he leaves his parked car. He's carrying lots of production notes and a brief case and also has a pipe in his hand. He clamps the pipe firmly in his teeth and crouches down tries to retrieve the fiver. He's struggling now and drops all his paperwork on the rain sodden floor of the car park, and we are rolling up laughing on the roof.

He hears us laughing and curses his unseen tormentors. We are all in the Club Bar later. I approach the counter to buy a pint. He's there telling the Club Steward how he intends to find out who pulled a fast one on him and get them sacked. He didn't.

I got some great training at the BBC and was now more rounded as an engineer, adding controls, heating and ventilation, and standby power generators to my electrical, refrigeration and air conditioning experience.

We were all sent away to The National Health Service's Hospital Engineering Centre in Falfield, near Bristol.

It was here that I got the theoretical training to add some science to the on-the-job training I got with Trollopes as an air conditioning engineer. I really enjoyed the training.

To break up the class-based sessions, the tutors would take us on some field trips. On the refrigeration course, they took us to Abergaveny Hospital.

On the way, we stopped off at a local pub for lunch and a few beers. By the time we got off the coach at the hospital gates we were all dying for a pee, but we couldn't find a toilet in the grounds.

We split up to find one. I did. But Chris Gibbons one of my BBC pals found himself unwittingly in the Venereal Disease clinic. Chris had a bit of a nancy boy way about him and I could just imagine him running around, clutching himself and shouting at the top of his voice, "Excuse me, is there a flipping toilet in here, mate?", to all the chaps trying to keep a low profile in the pox clinic.

Anyway, Chris is late catching up with the group and we have now made our way down to the morgue. The hospital engineer has warned us all of what we are about to see. Most of the hospital engineers on the course will have to maintain the refrigerated cabinets in their morgues, which is why we have all been brought here. This was new to me as I only look after the air conditioning at the Beeb, of course.

Anyway, we pass through the morgue and all the tables on which all the bodies are dissected, and we are now staring wide-eyed into the fridges.

There are bodies on stretchers in there, three high. The one at the bottom has his blue feet facing out the door and there is a brown paper label tied to his big toe with his name on it.

Some of the guys are feeling a bit squeamish now. Not me, because I'd seen my Dad and Mum dead and I am a trained first aider. The whole place reminded me of our staff kitchen at 3 am in the morning when no is around except us maintenance engineers.

But, just at this point, Chris Gibbons finally catches up with us, but he has had no warning of what we were all looking at.

"Fuck me, Dave", he says breathlessly, having run down the ramp to the basement. "I only ended up in the pox clinic; everyone was hiding behind their newspapers and wouldn't tell me where the pisshole was".

He then takes a good look around his new surroundings and says in my ear. "What have I missed? Is it a freezer or a fridge or what?"

"Er ...Fridge", says I, trying to keep a straight face. "But I don't think it's working right and the meat is going off in the bottom…look down there"

Chris goes down on his haunches to take a good look at the problem.

He then spots 10 blue toes poking out of a sheet with a label on one them and falls back onto his arse in shock.

Well, I nearly wet myself!

Having a BBC photo pass was handy too. I used to walk into the Boxing arenas like the Albert Hall show my pass and tell them I was with the OB team (Outside Broadcasting team) and wanted to come in for a piss. It always worked and I hardly ever bought a ticket for any fights again while I was at the Beeb.

1980
Mrs. Right, nearly dies

"I woke her, not knowing, as yet, if she could hear me
or answer me or if she could move. She blinked and
reached out to me and told me that she loved me".

But just as life couldn't get any better Maria had a massive brain haemorrhage and nearly died. If fact, she was given the last rites in hospital before an emergency operation to seal the blood vessel that was leaking into her brain. She thought she had a choice and said yes to this operation, when, in fact, she had none at all.

The surgeon shook both Maria's parents and my hands and said. "I'm glad she is going down for this operation in a positive mood. We are working in an extremely dangerous area for her. If she pulls through.... she may be blind, lose some speech and may be paralysed....but she is in good hands and we'll do our best for her". He patted my shoulder and walked away from us. I nearly fell over.

I kissed her goodnight and went to Pat's and Bobby's flat on the Isle of Dogs and I cried my eyes out like a child. I wasn't sure I'd ever see her again.

I went back to the hospital the next day and met Maria's parents again. Maria's Mum, Eileen, shook the hand I offered her and said. "I don't like men with beards; it's a sign of laziness..." I thought, she is going to be a barrel of laughs. I stayed the night in a chair in the hospital waiting room and the doctors woke me in the morning to say I could see her.

"She's asleep, so you'll have to wake her", the nurse said. I went into the recovery room and couldn't believe what I saw. Maria was as white as a sheet, with tubes going in and out of her head and arms, and her whole head was covered in a bandage like a turban.

I woke her, not knowing, as yet, if she could hear me or answer me or if she could move. She blinked and reached out to me and told me that she loved me.

She could see, she could hear, she could talk, she could move. I told her to rest and I'd be back later. The nurse handed me all the shoulder length hair they had taken from her before the op (I said I'd get a wig made from it) and I ran down the stairs ten at a time and called her parents to tell them. I was ecstatic.

She came back to intensive care and it was looking really good for her. She was on steroids and had grown some light hair on her face, had a bald head and a twitch on one side of her face and was being spoon-fed food when I proposed to her.

She accepted and told the rest of ward who cheered from their beds.

I'd joke for years that "I proposed to her on her death bed and then she went and lived"!

She recovered well and I was invited to go on holiday to Ireland with her and her parents and her younger brother David. Despite my cockney/Irish upbringing, I'd never been to Ireland and so I looked forward to this immensely and was not disappointed.

I went over for a week, taking the Spitfire with me. Maria's Dad was from the Irish countryside in County Carlow and the car caused a bit of a stir locally when I got there and I enjoyed the notoriety.

We stayed in the house that Henry, Maria's Dad, and his ten brothers and sisters grew up in.

It was like going back in time to my youth in the 1950's. Everyone was so polite and people spoke to each other as they passed in the street. It took me a while to settle down to the slower pace.

I was back to having only one socket outlet in the kitchen again, and the fridge and the telly were plugged into that, so you could not use anything else electrical without causing a real problem.

There was no running water in the house and you had to go down the country lane outside and use the hand pump by the side of the road and fill up a few buckets and bring them back twice a day.

There was a big range in the kitchen for cooking and it supplied some hot water too.

There was no bathroom though. There was an external toilet but it did not have any flush cistern in there or a sewer pipe from it.

Henry said that we could use it if you wanted to but you have to dispose of the slop bucket at the end of the holiday. He went for a crap in the field next door instead.

This was just like being down Hop picking again, thirty years earlier.

I took Maria's Granddad for a fast drive down the country lanes to his local pub in the Spitfire with the roof down. He didn't bat an eyelid. He walks into the pub, which is full of farmers and their sheep dogs. One asked what he's been up to and he says, "I've just been taking a racing car for a test drive".

"Right…what'll ya have?" they say, equally unimpressed.

"I'll have the same as John", says I.

"Two brandy and Lucozades, please!" I find this hilarious, but that's what they serve, and the Lucozade came in little mineral bottles just like tonic water does.

"You'll have to excuse me …but in England we only drink Lucozade when we are sick", I explain.

Up jumps a scruffy farmer and he tells me, "You see, the English think we are thick…but while the Brandy is making you sick…the Lucozade is making you well again."

Brilliant. I nearly wet myself laughing.

Maria's Dad was a real comedian and a right character. He and I would go out shooting rabbits and bring them back to the house. We'd go to the sheep and cattle marts too. I really took to Ireland and Maria's family and they took to me too.

I wasn't their first choice, as I'm sure they would have preferred Maria to marry a church going Irishman. But I won them over in time.

Henry was a night sleeping car attendant and did decorating jobs on his off days for a local Jewish businessman.

I proposed to Maria again in the upstairs restaurant in the Prospect of Whitby in Wapping. I'd tricked her with a cheap birthday card, and she was unaware I'd ordered a bottle of Champagne and had a huge card behind the scenes and her engagement ring in my pocket. I went down on one knee and proposed to her, and everyone in the restaurant cheered and clapped.

A large American woman turned to her husband and said, "George, did you hear what the Brit just did? My God wasn't that romantic?" I felt great.

How strange it was to be doing this in the same historic pub that, 20 years before, I used to scrounge money outside of, minding cars.

Maria couldn't see the benefits of living in the derelict docks I loved. I knew that Wapping would become the place to be in the future but she would not have it. It was a real wrench to move from there, but I also knew it would get me away from the nightlife distractions that the pubs offered.

Many of my friends were having marital problems and I wanted to avoid that at all costs. I was 30 years of age now and wanted to settle down and have kids of my own.

I still wanted to keep in touch with my pals and there was no way I would abandon Rob or my roots anyway. But I now did not have to be in Wapping 24/7. It wasn't the same place I knew.

1982
Wedding bells

"I loved the whole day, and my late Mum came too.
I kept a photograph of her with me all day."

Doing shift work at the BBC was handy as it allowed me and Henry (Maria's Dad) time to spend a year renovating entirely a tiny 2 bedroomed terrace house in St Stephens Road in Enfield. The house was 15 miles from Wapping and my family and cost us £21,500.

On 26 July, 1982, Maria and I were married in Arnos Grove in New Southgate, North London, in the parish where Maria's mother, father and brother were living.

To make sure my family and East End pals were not inconvenienced (and to make sure they came) I arranged for two coaches to bring them all to the wedding, the party afterwards and to take them home after it too.

Maria's parents paid for the hall and the dinner and I paid for the bar.

I'd ordered all the wine, spirits and the draught beer pumps and coolers from my pal Gary Ayris's warehouse in Wapping, as he gave me a discount.

I had to travel down to Wapping from Enfield on the morning of the wedding to get it all and bring my Best Man, Robert, back to Enfield. It poured down and, when I got to the warehouse in my little disco van, it suddenly dawned on me that I could not get everything back in one trip and now had make two return journeys.

When Gary put the first load onto my little white Honda truck, the suspension sank to the floor and I couldn't see the wheels anymore.

This meant I would have to travel four times through 13 miles of shopping crowds on a Saturday morning. It was raining "stair rods" too. I did it, but turned up in right state just minutes before the wedding.

It stopped raining in the middle of the service and a great ray of sunshine shone through a stain glass window onto Maria and me and I knew that was Mum sending her approval.

We had a traditional three-piece Irish band provide the music at the party and two blind telephonists from Barclays played their guitars and sung a few songs with their guide dogs at their feet too. No disco!

I loved the whole day, and my late Mum came too. I kept a photograph of her with me all day. Rob broke the habit of a lifetime and wore a suit and a tie. He looked great in it too. He caused a bit of a stir when one of the bridesmaids went missing and had to be dragged off the coach just as it left. He had convinced her to go back his flat in Wapping with him.

At the end of the evening Maria and I went back to our new home for the first time together. I carried her over the threshold and she started crying. She was already missing her family and her dog, Sheba.

We had started a completely new life. With Maria away from her parents and her brother David and I was a long way from my family, the Docks and Wapping.

We woke the next day and drove to Luton and stayed overnight in a Hotel local to the airport. Maria had no idea where I'd booked our honeymoon at all.

We woke up late and had to run through the airport following a hostess to make the plane. I told her where we were going just as we took off.

We arrived in The Hilton Sorrento Palace to a floral display and the champagne on ice that I'd ordered in our room.

We had a great holiday, and, to cap it all, Italy won the World Cup while we were there. Maria and I watched the final on one of the many TV's now especially installed in the hotel bar.

As each goal went in, everyone would run to the hotel windows and watch a massive firework display over the Bay of Naples. We later went down to the main square, La Piazza Tatso in Sorrento and clambered on board the back of a farmer's truck and paraded around the town on it. People were passing cakes and wine up to us as we waved the Italian flag. It was fabulous.

We later visited the old Sorrento fishing village and vowed to ourselves that we would miss an evening meal in our grand hotel and dine out in one of the restaurants by the sea in the tiny marina. We encouraged another couple to come with us and do the same.

When we eventually made our way down the back streets, we found the marina area deserted and virtually closed for the night. There was a family sitting outside their restaurant and I asked them where everyone was.

"We only open in the daytime as no-one comes down here at night" was the answer.

Anyway, they said they couldn't turn us away hungry and turned on the lights and cooked us a fabulous meal. We met the whole family, which included Peppini (Josephina) their disabled teenage daughter. She had one normal leg but the other terminated with a foot where her knee should be. They were praying for an operation to correct it.

20 years later Maria and I returned to Naples on a Mediterranean cruise. We jumped into a taxi and sped from Naples to Sorrento and went back to find that tiny restaurant by the tiny marina.

We introduced ourselves and asked if the same family ran the business still, and they did. Even the elderly mother of the family who cooked the meal all those years ago came out to her window to wave to us.

Sadly, Peppini did not get her operation. It was brittle bone disease that had afflicted her so badly.

"So, anyway...can we have lunch today?" I asked.

"No, sorry", they said. "These days, we only open in the evening and not in the daytime...look there's the people carrier we have bought to bring everyone down from the main square."

But the owner took us up to the Sorrento Palace Hotel we honeymooned in 20 years earlier and bought us a drink to thank us for looking them up again.

You couldn't make it up could you?

We loved our new life together but on Sundays Maria would go home to her parent's house for Sunday dinner, and I'd go to Wapping for a few beers with the lads and then back to my sister Pat's house, in Stepney Green, for my dinner.

The Exley family centred on Pat now and her home, and she took on the role of Matriarch to us all, and Rob and I loved her for that.

I was getting fairly independent now, as I had also been living on my own for some time. So I could cook a bit, do the shopping, washing, ironing and stuff. This was all a bit new to Maria, though, as her Mum did all that for her. So I had to teach her how to do it.

She took to it really well, but, if there were any guests to entertain for dinner, that was different.

We asked her friend Liz to come round for tea one night. This was to become known as "the upside down pies night".

I kept Liz entertained in the front room while Maria heated up some pies and fried some chips in the kitchen. After an hour, I went into the kitchen to find her running around it with the oven mitts on fire, and she pushed me out of the room to hide her embarrassment.

After another 30 minutes I went back again and asked what was taking her so long. It turns out she'd taken the steak and kidney pies out of their tin foils and put them on a baking tray, only for them to flatten out to a sort of mush.

I explained she needed to cook them in their little tin foil trays, really. So she now set out to spoon them back into the tin trays. When I went back in again, she was struggling as the crusty pastry was now at the bottom of the tin foil trays instead of the top. So she'd sprinkled cheese on them and was now browning them off.

Some new chips were required now, too, as the others had got burnt along with the oven mitts.

So after two and a quarter hours we sat down to eat upside down meat pies au gratin and chips and we didn't stop laughing all night. Maria was worn out, poor cow. She did go on to be a great cook and hostess after that, though.

I used to love playing tricks on Maria and would creep into the house and frighten the shit out of her. I climbed up the side of the house once and peered into the bathroom window once just to scare her for a laugh.

I came close to winning the lottery once, so I just altered two figures and brought the ticket to Barclays at Finsbury Park where she worked. When I told her in the street, she was skipping for delight and I joined in. She didn't think it was as funny as I did when I told her the truth, though.

Maria fancied the idea of driving, so took lessons and passed first time. Parking was never her strong point, and she'd arrive home at St Stephen's Road and leave the car running in the middle of the road for me to park. I'd bought her a nice little red Metro from a car sale, which she loved.

I was changing as a person now I was married. Maria had great faith in me, and was telling me I was different from my old pals. I couldn't see what she meant by that and didn't really want to be any different anyway.

I was now no longer just the electrician that I'd set my early target to be in the mid 1960's. I was also a shift team leader, and people were starting to see me as Supervisor material.

I wanted to see how far I could get in my life, despite the poor start I had been handed. I can recall sitting in a rooftop plant room with a team colleague, Peter Singfield. I was training Peter how to charge refrigerant gas into one of the main cooling plants.

Peter has reminded over the years that he asked me where I saw myself in 5 years time. Apparently my answer was "I am going to be a Building Services Manager just like our boss, Andrew Galloway, and have my own building to manage".

Five years later that is exactly what happened.

Maria and I discussed having a family. I was 34 years old now and did not want to leave it too long. She fell pregnant the moment we stopped taking precautions. I can still recall our delight at viewing the pregnancy test kit result and our amazement at the confirmation call from the GP.

Kelly Kathleen Exley was born on the 26th November, 1986, in Chase Farm Hospital in Enfield. Because of Maria's medical history, the hospital advised her to have a caesarean section. This was problematical and she had a very bad infection as a result.

We were delighted to have a first baby, but this was not as easy as it looked in the baby food adverts. Kelly would not sleep through the night for the next 13 months and we were exhausted. Having to work nights was killing me - I needed a new career on days.

We were starting to find the our first home, a two bedroomed terraced house, far too small for all the paraphernalia that surrounds a first child, and concluded it was time to leave St Stephen's Road.

We found the next best house we could afford at that time. It was a semi-detached, three bedroomed former council house on a mixed housing development. Nice house at the time. But somehow I never thought of it as our last move.

The bathroom was off the kitchen, which reminded me of my days in Riverside Mansions in Wapping somewhat.

Maria gave me the task of improving that bathroom. I'd installed a bidet in the last house and she was missing the luxury of that. The 70's avocado suite had to go too.

So I packed her and Kelly off to Ireland one Easter and started ripping the bathroom to pieces the Thursday night they left. It was a long and arduous weekend with no water or toilet in the house.

Once I'd got the room cleared, I found out that we could not house the bidet without changing the layout somewhat. So I had to disconnect the central heating radiator, raise the bath and relocate the toilet and its sewage pipe to flow away under the bathtub.

I finally finished it all at 2 am on the Tuesday morning after the Bank Holiday, and sank into my new bath full of bubbles and raised a large glass of whisky and ice to a job well done. My arms were cut to ribbons and I was exhausted.

I woke when I heard Maria and Kelly come through the door in the late afternoon. I sat up to try and catch her gushing praise as she entered her new bathroom for the first time.

Her first words were. "Well, I'm not having that; that's just ridiculous!" I was gutted and went out for a long walk. I did come back. The following Easter, I took it all apart again and rearranged it just how she wanted it.

1986–1990
The Broadgate years

*"Prince Charles came to open the estate and we were
entertained by Olympic Ice Skating Champions, Torvil
and Dean, who danced all their marvellous routines for
us, including Bolero".*

My way forward at the BBC was barred by staff with more years served than I had. "The Jackers Journal", The London Evening Standard newspaper, had come up trumps and I saw my next opportunity for advancement and responded to an advert for a maintenance supervisor.

I left the Beeb after 6 happy years to join Rosser and Russell as a day shift working maintenance supervisor at Broadgate. It was, at the time, the biggest and best new office development in London since the Barbican site was developed.

Broadgate, a 32 acre (129,499 m2) office and retail estate in the City of London, is now owned by British Land and managed by Broadgate Estates. The original developer was Rosehaugh Stanhope, it was built by Bovis Construction (I'd go on to cheekily nickname them Bogus Construction!) and it was the largest office development in London until the subsequent arrival of the first stage of the Canary Wharf development in the early 1990s.

This modern and mainly-pedestrianised development was being built on the original site of Broad Street railway station (closed in 1986) and beside, and above, the railway approaches into Liverpool Street station.

There would be 3,900,000 ft² of office floor space; retail and leisure accommodation spread over the site, and over 30,000 office staff would be employed there.

My colleagues at the Beeb thought I was mad and told me I should not leave. I'd heard this before when I planned to leave Trollopes. So I thought I'd take the chance to reach my full potential, whatever it would be, and left.

This was to prove to be a fantastic career move for me, just as I hoped it would. I saw it as a way of moving quickly from the maintenance contractors to the client's own management team and it worked.

The job entailed taking management of the first building to be completed in the whole development and maintaining it for an American Express backed stockbroker firm called Shearson Lehman Bros.

It was now 1986 and Big Bang had just turned the City markets upside down. The Stock Exchange had been de-regulated. Out went the old boy network and in came the East End wide boy traders with their computers and mobile phones, and there was no going back for me either.

American Express had bought out a London company called Messells Ltd ahead of Big Bang so they were could hit the ground running.

I was leading a shift team and moving into management.

Unfortunately, one of the lads from the BBC followed me. A Geordie fitter from Hartlepool called Frank Sumpter.

There is a story that, during the days of the Napoleonic Wars, a sailing ship was wrecked off the coast of Hartlepool.

When the local Hartlepudlians boarded the ship, they found some monkeys and hanged them believing them to be foreign spies! So people from Hartlepool are known as "Monkey hangers", the people that hung the monkeys.

Frank was trouble and I needed him following me into this new job like I needed a sore head. He could be great company one minute and then screaming in your face the next. I'm sure he had a drug problem and he was very unpredictable.

I rearranged the shifts so that I didn't have to deal with him and the company later sacked him. I thought good riddance at the time. But he later died of a heart failure before he was 40 years old. I wasn't surprised but felt extremely sorry for him and his family.

The hand over of the building from the main contractors and the developer was predictably risky. It is always a difficult time as the plant is still being commissioned, and information, drawings, and operation and maintenance manuals are scarce.

Shearson's were very IT dependant, and the power and cooling to the computer rooms must stay operational whatever happens. This was where I could make my mark.

Shearson's Building Service Manager was a Jewish-Australian guy called Vic Crespin. Vic and I hit it off instantly. He had a great sense of humour and he was always pleased when I was in the building. He had great faith in me and knew, whatever happened, I'd sort things out while he concentrated on the move into the building.

I was carrying out a tour of the main cooling plant rooms and, when I opened the door, I found the whole place in chaos.

Imagine yourself in the boiler room of huge battleship ship and it's about to sink, and you're the ships engineer who is expected to go down with it.

The building's huge cooling tower pumps, chilled water pumps and the refrigeration chillers were all stopping and restarting every 10 secs or so. The noise was deafening. This meant that the main computer room temperature would be increasing and, before you know it, we would have an IBM mainframe computer meltdown.

This looked like a major Building Management computer control problem, so I made two calls. One to the controls site management team leader asking him to get his arse down here quick, and one to Vic Crespin, the Building Services Manager.

"Vic, can you pop down to the chiller room. I've got a little problem to show you". It was 5:30pm and everyone was going home, so I was lucky to get hold of anyone at all, really.

When Vic saw it all, he nearly fainted.

The controls man quickly threw all the plant control switches from "Auto" to "Manual" so that we had just one set of pumps and one set of chillers running. The cooling water temperatures all came back down again and we all sighed with relief. We were just about to go home when we suddenly heard a loud creaking sound.

No one could work out what was going on now. I started to feel the pipe work around the plant room as it sounded like the pipes were about to explode.

The cooling towers on the roof had stopped and we were about to lose all the plant again. So I then run up to the roof to throw their local controls switches from "Auto" to "Manual" to get them running too. They came on and a huge cloud of steam was ejected from the cooling towers across the main square of Broadgate.

We all gather by the main plant panel in the basement again and the controls expert now believes he knows what is wrong. The BMS computer is not recognising that the pumps have started, so it keeps changing them over.

He opens the panel up. It's full of wires, contactors, flashing lights, etc, and puts his hand straight onto a tiny glass fuse. He repairs it and puts all the switches back to "Auto" and everything goes back to working normal again.

This has impressed Vic and he now feels he owes me one.

The next day, he and I are strolling through the unfinished car park in the basement and he says, boastfully. "That's where I'm gonna park my car, mate", pointing to the best bay.

"And where do I park mine", I enquire.

"Right next to mine", he answers. I thought, bloody hell, he is going to offer me the in-house management job I've set out to get. I'd hoped this is what would happen but did not expect it after just a couple of months.

A couple of days go by and Vic calls me to his office. I know what this is…he is going to ask to join his team. Right?

I walked in happy as Larry and he then introduces me to another person. "Dave Exley, meet David Westbrook. David is my new Assistant Building Services Manager"

Fuck me! I've had the promotional door slammed in my face again.

David turns out to be an old pal of his from Rashleigh Phipps. He's a nice bloke and we get on, but I still feel he still has taken my job away from me.

Ah well. If it's not to be, it's not to be.

A few months go by and David is starting to think he has taken on a bit more than he can handle. Both he and Vic are electrical biased whereas I am more of an all rounder and can understand both the Electrical and the Mechanical aspects of Building Services. I also have the experience needed to operate the Building Management System (BMS) computer.

Why the fuck did he take David on and not me, I thought. So I'll give these two my support and who knows what might happen.

It doesn't take long before I get my next chance to impress.

There is an alarm coming from the mainframe computer room on which the dealer desks rely. The business is wholly dependent on them and the main water chillers in the basement also directly cool these computers.

Shearson's are live on the world's markets and trading is heavy. These people make millions of pound per minute and they are about to get wiped off the market.

I set to work to find out what the hell is going on. The BMS computer is showing me that everything is working as it should. All the pumps are running so are all the chillers and the cooling towers. But the temperature of the water to and from the cooling towers is too high.

Vic is now inside the computer room and giving David and me anxious calls on the radio in his familiar Australian accent. He has lost his sense of humour now.

"Guys, if the water temperature goes up two more degrees…the IT director is going to turn off the mainframes and we are all out of a fucking job. Do something, and do it fucking quickly, for Christ sake!"

David is looking at me and he hasn't got a clue where to start.

"Right, let's go up to the roof," I said. There was another supervisor (a right jobs-worth) in the building with us. But he was worried about going near the cooling towers, as he did not have the confidence I had in our water treatment records and procedures. He was saying it was more than his job's worth to go up there. "Fine", I said. "You stay here, you prick, and I'll go up there".

Cooling towers have a notorious record as being the source of Legionnaire's Disease because they operate at the right temperature for the bacteria Legionella Pnuemophilla to grow in unacceptable numbers. The disease got its name when a large group of elderly army veterans died after the vapour from a poorly maintained cooling tower entered the fresh air supply to a hotel where their veteran's conference was being held.

They died of a pneumonia like chest infection for which there was no cure at the time.

Vic is back on the radio by the time I got to the roof. "It's now or never, guys. One more degree higher and we are all fucked..."

I opened the access panel on the side of the cooling tower and I could see straight away what the problem was. The base of the tower had 3 feet of scale deposits in it and this was blocking the tower water filter. This was starving the basement chillers of the cooling water they needed.

Whereas "the jobs-worth" supervisor had no confidence in what he was doing, I knew that the bacteria levels of the towers were under control. Clearly something else was wrong with the water treatment but we did not have any Legionnaires Disease issues to worry about.

I was dressed in a smart suit and tie. But time was running out. So I kicked off my shoes, threw off my jacket and climbed into the cooling tower.

I was up to my knees in water and hot water was raining down on me from above too. I undid the filter/strainer basket from the outlet pipe and watched as the water rushed down the empty pipe to the chiller plant in the basement again.

Yes, some of the scale went down there too, and I knew that would cause us some more grief, but not as much as a total lack of cooling water at all would.

The lads in the chiller room and Vic in the computer room all cheered as the temperature started to decrease. It was now all hands to the pumps in the basement, as we had to clean the filters out down there every twenty minutes or so to get all the crap that had come down from the cooling towers, but that was running clear after a couple of hours.

The dealers on the trading floor didn't get to hear how close they were to being off the world's markets, but the story of my heroics went down well with Shearson's management.

Within a few days, I was asked to go for a drink in a local pub, The Red Lion, with Vic and Dave. Vic offered me a job as his 2nd Assistant Building Services Manager alongside David Westbrook.

David had apparently played a major part in it, saying that I knew more about the Building Services in the building than he did.

I was now no longer a contractor, no longer an oily rag supervisor, but part of the management of a large investment bank. I was on my way up the greasy pole of success again.

Vic and Dave and I became great friends and spent many a happy hour in the Red Lion. I called it the Lyon Rouge whenever I told anyone where we were going for a few jars, so as not to give the game away.

When the Broadgate Estate was almost complete, all the building managers were invited to the official opening of the estate's open-air ice skating rink. It was right outside our building in the Broadgate Circle.

Prince Charles came to open the estate and Olympic Ice Skating Champions, Torvil and Dean, who danced all their marvellous routines for us, including Bolero, entertained us. It was a fantastic day, and we were served pink champagne and canapés by silver-service staff in donkey jackets.

I remember saying to Vic that I thought I should go back to work at about 3:30pm and he said. "Dave, mate, these things don't happen often; take it all in. Relax and enjoy yourself. You deserve it.".He was right and I did.

Vic had some great sayings he used to recite around lunchtimes and they stayed with me and I use them myself today.

For instance, when it was lunchtime, he'd say in his Aussie accent:

"Right mate, we've gotta eat now, 'cos if you don't eat; yer can't shit; and if yer can't shit; you'll die! Yer don't wanna die, do yer?"

At the end of lunch, he'd signal it was time to go back by saying, "Right, I didn't get where I am today by sittin' around 'ere all day".

I really enjoyed my time with Shearsons, and one day in particular stays with me.

There had been a legionnaire's disease scare on the estate and we were carrying out more water tests than usual. So I'd ordered a new batch of dip slides. These were sample test tubes with a dip slide, an agar plate suspended from a red cap that sealed the test tube. The dip slide was dipped in the water to be tested and then returned to the test tube. Bacteria was grown on the agar plate over a few days and compared to a chart to indicate if any bacteria were in your cooling tower. This told you how well your water treatment controls were working.

The new batch of test tubes arrived but they were the wrong sort. Instead of cooling tower tubes, I've been sent urine sample test tubes!

Well. We had a very lairy IT colleague who was showing too much interest in our cooling tower management, and he had generally too much to say for himself.

He came into the office and asked what we were doing to keep the disease from our building. I thought, gotcha!

"Actually, providing you can keep this confidential, you could help us," I say. "Sure, what have I got to do?" he comes back. So I pass him one of the urine sample kits and tell him to read it and get back to me later with a sample. But I remind him that he is not to tell a soul about it. Off he goes, and Dave and I are wetting ourselves laughing.

We come back from the "Lyon Rouge", suitably relaxed after sharing a bottle of Chardonnay, to find our colleague had filled the test tube with piss and left it on my desk. We were in fits again.

So I take the tube and sling the contents away down a loo. I then take a spare one to the vending area and fill it with tomato soup and take it back to my desk. Silly bollocks, Colin, the IT guy, returns two hours later to ask me if he is clear of Legionnaire's Disease or not.

"Where's the sample", I says. "Right there on your desk", he says, looking concerned. So I hold it up to the light and show him. By now the tomato soup has separated into two halves. Its red at the bottom and pink at the top, where Colin had left it yellow of course. So I shake it up and tell him it doesn't look good for him!

"Ever done this before, mate?" I ask. "Never", he says.

"So no one has ever taken the piss out of you before then?" I enquire, trying unsuccessfully to hide a grin.

The penny finally drops and he cracks up. He couldn't believe he'd been taken in. He'd covered his trouser in piss trying to fill the test tube too. You couldn't make it up, could you? Great fun.

I was keen to learn as much as I could about all the new systems in the building but our commissioning engineer, a miserable bastard called

Nick, just wouldn't let me.

But he'd left all his commissioning documents lying in the security room one night. So I photocopied every last word of them and put them back where I found them all. I read them back to front over the next few weeks and then I knew everything he did and never looked back.

I did the same with all the Operation and Maintenance Manuals for the building and became a font of information of all the building's critical systems.

First Aid at work and everywhere else

"I could see that his head was facing the wrong way from the rest of his body. So were his broken legs and arms. It was a very distressing scene, but I was not panicking".

"I knew my little first aid kit was not going help me much here. This was going to need real street medical procedures. So I just knelt on it to protect my old knee injury from the hard tarmac surface and got to work".

The first aid skills that I had initially picked up at the BBC were about to be severely put to the test. The BBC was great for providing additional training like this and they have come in handy a few times over the years.

I was still travelling down to Wapping from Enfield on Sundays for a few pints with the lads after Maria and I had married. One Sunday, I decided I'd start the lunchtime session off with a few jars in St Patrick's Social Club.

The usual familiar faces were in there with a crowd of younger Wappingites supporting the bar and the old gits sitting around the bar, as usual, talking about the old days. I loved this place.

Above the bar hung a number of snare drums from the Wapping Catholic Procession Band, old photos populated the other walls and it was business as usual with old Dockers calling out "Alright Davey boy, how's things?"

I'm into my second pint of lager when I spot one of the old boys is in trouble. You get an eye for things like this when you have been trained as well as I had been.

Old Mike is looking a bit rough and is holding his neck. His mates are oblivious to this as they are old now, and a bit pissed too.

I make my way over to him and take the pint out of his hand and try to talk to him, but he has passed out now.

So I push a few of his pals out of the way and ease him onto the floor. To all intents and purposes he's just fainted to his mates. But he is not responding to my calls and I can see his eyes are fixed and his lips are starting to turn blue.

I shout out for someone to call an ambulance. The head barman comes over and I tell him to say that we have an elderly man in cardiac arrest.

I now go into full resus mode and I'm giving this dear old man mouth-to-mouth resuscitation. I know I'm doing it properly as I had attended a refresher course within the last few weeks.

But I'm starting to struggle as old Mike has had quite a lot to drink and I was starting to gag. I send one of the younger lads over to Wapping River Police station to ask for help and a bottle of oxygen.

Mike suddenly shouts straight into my face, which takes me by surprise as I'm convinced he is dead and I'm trying to get him back.

I check for a pulse but there is nothing. This was Mike expelling my own air back through his vocal cords only.

The police arrived, but I'd been more successful by myself so I carried on. At last, the cavalry arrive and two ambulance men are at my side. I show them what I have been doing and they wrap Mike up and get him away to the London Hospital.

I fear the worse for him but everyone was amazed at what I'd done and wanted to buy me a drink. I couldn't face one right then and said I needed to get some fresh air.

I wandered over Wapping High St to the river park next to police station and sat and stared at the Thames for ten minutes to get over the shock of what had just happened and what I been through.

I wished for a moment that I'd never been trained and that way I could have looked the other way instead of trying to give mouth to mouth to a dead body that was vomiting stale beer back at me while I was trying to breathe life back into it.

That feeling was quickly replaced by one of pride in what I had just done and I went off to my sister Pat's for a well-earned Sunday Roast.

The next Sunday, I went back to St Pats to find out if Mike had survived his ordeal. Sadly, he hadn't and was pronounced dead shortly after he arrived at the London Hospital. He'd died of a massive heart attack and had no chance.

His family threw their arms around me and thanked me for giving him a chance. I felt sad but very proud and we all had a few beers together.

Being a first aider (I rather use the term First Responder) means you are obliged to react whenever there is a medical problem. If fact you become far more alert to these situations than others and you can never ever be just a bystander. You are the first to react and roll your sleeves up and get stuck in.

I maintained my interest in first aid after I joined Shearson Lehman and

I was called upon again one day to put my old skills into practice.

I was travelling between floors in the Broadgate building when I received a call on my mobile phone.

It was security. "Could you come down to the main security room? We have someone with a serious injury". Yeah, right, I thought. Someone's got a nasty scratch, maybe. This is an office block, not some hazardous factory.

I made my way down to the ground floor and entered the security room to find one of our maintenance contractors, George Ling, sitting in a chair, looking a little shocked with a crowd around him.

"Hello, George, what have you done then?" George stands up, whips off the towel that was covering his hand and shuts "I've cut my thumb off, David, I cut my bloody thumb off."

I go straight into action and sit him down and elevate his hand and, in a very calm voice, I say to him. "Ok…you've lost it now… there's nothing we can do about that now…so just sit still for me, all right?"

Inside me, though, I was panicking like hell and my head is spinning and my only thoughts are "Fucking hell. He's cut off his fucking thumb. What the hell am I gonna do?"

Surprisingly, there was little blood now. It was a clean chop and, by keeping his hand way above his head, I stopped any blood from spurting out. He tells me he grabbed a drive belt to stop a huge fan from continuing to turn after he'd switched it off, so that he could get on with his work a little quicker. I sent one of the other maintenance guys off to retrieve his thumb from the machine.

I bandaged him up and sent him of in an ambulance, holding in his good hand a severed thumb in a glass of iced water.

Poor George, they could not sew it back on. But he did return to work albeit a little handicapped.

These were pretty traumatic incidents, but the worse incident was to come.

Maria and I took a cheap holiday camp with some friends of ours. I wasn't in great form, didn't like the place and couldn't wait to get home and get my career back on track again.

On the way home, we are driving along a motorway in heavy traffic when suddenly I saw something flying through the air a hundred yards or so ahead of me.

It looked like one of those shredded lorry tyres you seen lying on the side of the motorway. It was spinning wildly in the air at about the height of a semi-detached house.

A the cars ground to a halt and, peering ahead, I could see people getting out of their cars and staggering around in shock.

So as usual, I get out of my car and go to see if I can help, after picking up my little first aid kit from the glove compartment and making my way through the stationary motorway traffic.

There are people by the side of the road vomiting and crying, and a man in jeans standing over the crumpled body of a young man.

I bend down to check for breathing and the guy standing above says "He's dead, mate, leave him".

The guy who is pronouncing this poor sod dead tells me he is a paramedic in the army.

There's no sign of life from this poor chap on the floor.

He's bare-footed, longhaired and I couldn't make out how he came to be there. Did he fall from a car?

The bystander repeats his advice to me as I bend down and I reply. "Thanks, mate, but if he is dead, I can't hurt him any more, can I?

It turns out this poor man had been running across the motorway and was hit by a number of vehicles. It wasn't a shredded tyre flying through the air. It was this guy who is now lying in front of me like a dead cat.

He looked dead all right. His eyes were fixed and staring straight ahead. But it was only seconds ago that he was alive and well, before he was hit by the cars. So, if anyone could save him, I thought I could.

I could see that his head was facing the wrong way from his torso. So were his broken legs and arms. It was a very distressing scene, but I was not panicking.

I knew my little first aid kit was not going help me much here. This was going to need some real street medical procedures. So I just knelt on it to protect my old knee injury from the hard tarmac surface and got to work.

Think, David, think. Then it came back to me. ABC, Airway, Breathing, Circulation.

The fact that his neck was twisted so badly could have been restricting his breathing. So I gently lifted his head and turned it slowly to face the right way.

This had an immediate effect and a spurt of air and blood flew from my patient's mouth and his chest started to heave and he was gasping noisily.

I stood up in shock and the bystander ran off but returned quickly with a huge plastic box full of medical provisions. I think he regretted his premature diagnosis of instant death.

This guy was still in trouble but at least he now had a fighting chance.

We set about securing his broken limbs so that he could be transported quickly to hospital. We both suspected he had a pneumothorax; a collapsed lung to you, as his breathing was very laboured and one sided.

It seemed like hours rather than minutes, but the Police, who had started directing traffic around us as I tended to this poor sod, eventually joined us. I was hoping they would take over from me, but no chance.

Shortly after that an ambulance team arrived and I gave them the history of what I'd found and done; and in seconds my patient was in the back of the ambulance and gone.

I was standing there covered in this guy's blood and in total shock and shaking from head to toe. But I'd just saved someone's life.

The Police could see I was in a state and took me back to my car. Maria had no idea about what I'd just gone through.

The coppers said they would stop the traffic and let me get off home and they did.

I was still in shock and not saying much as I set off down the motorway, our car now completely on its own.

After a mile, I was able to explain what I'd just experienced and I burst into tears and had to pull over on to the hard shoulder.

Maria drove us home while I got myself together.

To this day, I have always wondered if that poor sod lived or died. I have also been wondering if indeed he was trying to kill himself on the motorway that day.

I've consoled myself all these years that I just did the right thing, and that I was there at the right time for him.

1989
Joining Acuma

*"I'd come home and burst into tears in Maria's arms.
I felt a failure and that I could not cope".*

It's now approaching Christmas 1988 and I'd put on a bit of weight. I'd given up playing football many years earlier with my knee injury and was enjoying the Friday night pub life of the City again with my new workmates at Shearsons.

The London Marathon had by now become established as an annual event and we looked forward to it coming through the East End each year. The local roads on the route were closed off early on those Sunday mornings, which created a bit of nuisance, but, whether you liked or not, it was here to stay.

I thought I'd start jogging to lose some weight and put in an entry form for the race and managed to get in through the ballot.

My knee injury was still playing up but I found I could run in a straight line ok. I was able to run for about 45 mins and thought that would be ok. I ran the race on adrenaline only and didn't stop once for fear I'd never start again.

This was the hardest thing I had ever undertaken and I totally underestimated the stress and the exhaustion it would cause.

I used a psychological trick to help me through the race and just kept imagining myself at the finish straight, crossing the line and getting my medal whilst draped in one of the tin foil sheets that are handed to the cold and wet runners as they cross the line.

Don't ask me how I managed to complete it with such a poor training regime and a wonky knee, but I got to the finish line on the South side of Westminster Bridge.

As I approach the finish line absolutely exhausted, there were two veteran women runners just ahead of me. I now had a choice to make. I'd been told to wave my arms in the air at the finish as someone takes you photo and sends it to you.

If I was to cross the line in under 5 hours, they'd be in the shot, if I held back a bit, I'd go over the 5 hour time. So I gritted my teeth and raced on to lose the two old girls and finish in 4 hours 59 mins and 15 secs!

How the hell I thought 45 minutes running would have been enough I'll never know. I was crippled with blisters, aching all over and had broken two toenails off. This race was completed on sheer determination only. I raised £2,500 for charity too.

I got to the changing room (a single-decker bus) and could not get my trousers on. I had to lie down next to someone else and together we pulled each other's trousers up.

I sent the Cancer Macmillan nurses £1,500 in memory of my Dad and also took £1,000 up to St Joseph's Hospice and handed it over in cash to the manager.

I vowed I'd never, ever do it again. But I did it again, and again. Ten times in all!

I was still with Shearsons when they became Shearson Lehman Hutton but was starting to get itchy feet again. I'd created a position at the firm for a friend, Peter Singfield, to join me from the BBC and he settled into a similar supervisor's role that I had with Rossers.

Pete was on his way up too and it wasn't long before he was spirited away to join Norwich Union as Building Service Manager at a large office development in Aldgate. So he actually beat me to becoming a manager; you'll remember he and I had that discussion about "where we saw each other in five years time " when we were at the Beeb.

Vic had always fancied a role like our Facilities Director, Bob Hines, had at Shearsons. He was getting frustrated and would leave to join an oil company in the United Bank of Switzerland (UBS) building next door to us at Broadgate.

So, when I was asked to consider joining another wing of American Express as their Facilities Manager I jumped at it.

This was a new venture for Amex and they had taken over a personal finance company called Devonshire Financial Services (DFS) and were about to launch a new company called Acuma on the back of them.

I'd be working for a charming gentleman director and would go head first into fitting out buildings around the South East of England, including Tamesis their new head office in Egham, in Surrey.

I'd have to arrange all the moves, but my boss would take care of the new sales office move into Covent Garden.

I was really looking forward to this leap into Facilities Management and thought that, as this was a new company, I had nothing to beat and could pull this off. I was a little anxious about leaving the City of London for the first time in my career, but it was worth the risk.

Once again, I was told that I was making a huge mistake and should stay but I'd heard all this before and I was really keen to see how far I could go.

Someone once said, "Everyone rises to the level of his or her own incompetence". I didn't know it then but I was about to rise to mine.

We fitted out the Head Office in Egham, only for it to be burgled. My security guard was tied up and the intruders made off with £50,000 worth of computers and mobile phones.

I was managing "the office move" to Egham. It turned out that this was fifteenn different moves, but I completed them all. I arranged to meet my director at 6pm on the last Saturday night of the moves, at the Covent Garden office he was taking care of. The removals contractor in their lorry delivered me there. The boss was going to take me for a meal that night.

I'd been chasing him to make sure he picked up the Covent Garden office keys from the main contractors at the building hand over that day. He had them with him thank God.

However when we got up to the floor we had leased, there were no doors to secure the new offices from the rest of the building. They had not been fitted yet but were coming in the morning!

The director looks at me and I look at him. This is his baby and not mine. He asked me what he should do. So I take responsibility for his error and sit down on my briefcase in the middle of Covent Garden and phone every security company I know to try to get two guards to sit in the space for the next 48 hours.

"Do you think it's necessary?" the director asks.

"Look". I say. "We've just lost £50k worth of IT equipment from a locked office block in Egham and the M.D. is expecting to launch his business from here on Monday. I am not willing to walk away from all this new IT equipment, furniture and company files that's boxed and ready to go straight out of the building again, are you?"

He quickly agreed. We didn't get to go out for the meal though, as it was midnight before the guards turned up.

Driving to Egham every day from Enfield was killing me. I faced three hours in M25 traffic jams in the morning and three hours coming home again too.

I had a brand new company car, a really nice sporty Vauxhall, and a cheap company mortgage, but I was missing the City and all my mates and the support I'd previously had around me. I had to get up a 5am in the morning and go to bed as soon as I got in at 10pm at night. This was no way to live and I was getting depressed. I'd come home and burst into tears in Maria's arms. I felt a failure and that I could not cope.

Maria was fantastic about it. She told me that it was not worth the hassle and that I should leave and go back to the City again. The money was not important, and she loved me before when I was just an air conditioning engineer, and she didn't care about anything other than my health and happiness. She had confidence in me and said that I just need to go back a step or two to go forward again.

My pals at Shearsons rallied around me. They could hardly recognise the laughing and confident guy I once was and were sad to see me so down and unsure of myself.

Before I left them, I had put a successor in my place and now I wished I hadn't.

Mike Collier worked as mobile engineer and came to the building to provide shift cover holiday relief. He was made from the same stuff I was, and just like Vic and David, felt confident in me, I could only sleep well when Mike was covering one of the shift guys. I'd told Mike he needed to come in from the cold and take up a shift job, but he did not want lose his van. Mike subsequently took my advice and later became the Property Director at Lehman Bros at their new Canary Wharf offices.

But, in 1989, I'd put him into my job and here I was trying to get it back again. That could not happen.

I took Maria's and my close friends' advice and jacked in the job with Acuma before I went any more downhill.

I was told by many others I must be mad to leave Acuma but I knew this was the right thing to do. I bought the car from them at a knock down price and made a few phone calls around the City.

Dave Westbrook and I were having a few beers in the Lyon Rouge one Friday night with one of his old mates, Andy Steward. Andy reminded me of the London taxi driver who won Mastermind. We three got on really well, had the same sense of humour and loved a beer or three. We have remained good friends ever since.

1990
Joining Clifford Chance

"Keith would try to remind me at every salary review about the day I skipped down the steps of Blackfriars House like Fred Astaire when I got the job. I probably did too".

Dave Westbrook at Shearsons reminded me that one of the many organisations that came to see how we managed 1 Broadgate, were now taking a new building in the City. According to Dave they were very impressed with me at the time. No one had told me that at the time and I was happy at Shearson's at the time anyway.

So Dave gave me their details and said I should go and look at the building they were moving to.

When I do, the hairs on the back of my neck stand up. The building they are taking is about 500,000 square feet right in the heart of the City, at the Barbican end of London Wall.

The site is known as Little Britain (subsequently renamed 200 Aldersgate St) and the sole tenant will be Clifford Chance, a major firm of solicitors. They would be taking a fully repairing lease for 25 years.

The only concern I have is that the building looks about two years from completion. The concrete centre cores are erected but the steel work walls and floors are only now being erected.

Anyway I write to Keith Toms, their Head of Services and say that I understand they are recruiting an Engineering Services Manager for their new premises. They weren't, of course, but I was trying to plant a seed in their minds. I reminded them that they came to see me at Shearson Lehman Bros.

Basically, I'm telling them that they needed me and that I wanted to explore the mutual benefits of having me employed by them.

It worked and I'm lying in bed one morning and take a call from Keith's secretary, Kathy Saunders. She has a broader cockney accent than my own and Keith wants to find a mutual time for me to come in and see him.

I leap out of bed and tell Maria. I'm even more delighted as they are obviously not put off by cockney accents!

I'm to be interviewed by The Head of Services, his boss, General Manager, Keith Salway, and Bill Healy, the senior partner from Tuckers the Mechanical and Electrical Consultancy who were designing the systems for the new building.

I didn't care who they were going to put me up against. I felt my life depended on getting this job and I'd do anything to make sure I got it.

The main problem was that they weren't looking for anyone at this time. There was no job description, no advert to answer and no vacancy to fill.

The consultant checked me out technically and there was nothing he could catch me out on. So I was doing well. Mr Salway then says "I have one problem, we are not looking for anyone at this time and, if we did, it would not be for at least 18 months, anyway, when the building is completed"

I had to think quickly otherwise I'm out of the door and still out of work.

"That will be too late, Mr Salway" I replied. "You'll need your Building Services Manager on site now to ensure he knows the building inside outside by the time it opens. He needs to be there as the systems are being designed, installed and commissioned. He needs to be preparing your maintenance teams and service providers now to take on the building"

I pointed at Bill and said "Look with all due respect, these guys will be looking to drop the ball and pass the buck onto you guys as soon as the building is finished. Right, Bill? Well, I'm the guy who is going to catch that ball and run with it".

"Mmmm", says Mr Salway. "Ok. Look do something for me, would you, David? Would you write me a paper on what exactly you'll be doing for the next two years until the building is finished, and let me have that by the end of next week please?"

"I would do, but I'm going on leave to Ireland next week, and it's in the middle of nowhere so I don't have access to a computer", I reply.

"I'm sure you'll manage it somehow," says Mr Salway.

This is a test I need to pass.

So off we go to Maria's Mum and Dad's in Eire and I set about hand writing my business plan. Maria's brother, David, and his wife Ann were now living in Dublin. So I call them and establish that they have a computer. At least she'll be able to type up my scruffy notes into something more professional.

So they come out to the countryside to Sunday dinner and take my notes home with them and return the next week with a typed copy for me to send to Clifford Chance.

A week later, I am invited to another interview in Blackfriars House, again in London, with just Keith Toms who wastes no time in telling me that they are offering the job (that didn't exist) and wanting to know when I could start. It was for £5k more than I had been earning too!

I just couldn't believe my ears.

I remembered that there was a red phone box on the other side of the road from their meeting rooms and I ran straight over to call Maria. We were over the moon. Clifford Chance was the product of a merger in 1987 of two London based law firms, Clifford Turner and Coward Chance. I was joining the largest law firm in the world as the Building Services Manager for Little Britain, their brand new London office.

I was back on track and taking on an existing team that knew very little about modern buildings. This was a fantastic opportunity for me.

Keith would remind me at every salary review about the day I skipped down the steps of Blackfriars House like Fred Astaire when I got the job. I probably did too.

My first week was very memorable. I visited the 9 buildings that Clifford Chance was then occupying. Everyone was still talking in terms of either Coward Chance or Clifford Turner and not Clifford Chance and it reminded me of being back at Shearsons. In the early days there, everyone still spoke in terms of "Are you from Messells or are you from Shearsons?"

The Clifford Chance buildings were not in good shape and I thought I could make an instant impact by getting whatever poor air conditioning systems they had into some reasonable working order at least.

I was based at 14 New Bridge St, near Blackfriars Bridge, in London, and, when I returned to it after two days of building tours, a very unhappy colleague who was packing his belongings into a black plastic bag confronted me. He was the Office Manager and had just been fired. He just said, "Watch your back, mate", as he left.

I was stunned, as I understood we would be working together as a team. Keith called me in and said he had to fire him. He told me I'd be doing his job now. I wasn't happy with this and told him so.

I said I was here to concentrate on the new building and not be distracted by managing the maintenance teams they had at this time. He looked a little taken back but said he would work around this for the moment but I would be expected to inherit them at some stage.

The next day I was to visit one of our larger properties, Royex House, which overlooked the Guildhall, and Mrs Pat Berry who was our House Manager there.

She told me we had a very important meeting with the senior partner, Sir Max Williams, at the top of the building. Blimey, I'd never met a "Sir" before.

Sir Max was out on the fire escape at the top of the building. Pat was the firm's charity organiser too and she's spent the previous day filling hundreds of balloons with helium and tying return address tags on them.

Anyway she goes up to the roof and opens the door at the top of the stairs and says she will give us a shout at 10:00 hours exactly.

She does and Sir Max and I push all the balloons up the stairs and out on to the roof where they rise majestically across the city skyline and we all laughed and cheered them on their way.

I remember thinking…I'm going to like working here!

Over the next few weeks, the tags made their way back to the building and we learn that some balloons had made their way as far as Amsterdam!

Maria and I were still getting over the shock of how much your life changes when you have your first child and we were in no rush to repeat the sleepless nights or indeed her caesarean operation. But we thought it would be unfair for Kelly to grow up without a brother or a sister and all the extended family that would bring in her in later years. If there is no brother or sister, there are no nieces, nephews, etc. So we decided that, after a five-year gap, we were ready for another child. Enter Louise Ellen Exley on 14th April 1991.

Unlike Kelly, Louise ate better and should have slept through the nights as a result. But Lou had asthma and coughed and spluttered continuously and couldn't keep her milk down. So we had another miserable time with our second new born. Lou had to be ventilated with ventolin and used a nebuliser for most of her infant life. But the family was now complete and I loved being a Dad to the girls.

I joined the Little Britain project team and regularly visited the new site and I felt I was going to spend the rest of my career with Clifford Chance.

I managed to get all the old ventilation plant at Royex House and Blackfriars House working and everyone is impressed with what I'm doing for them. We had a potential Legionella scare at Tallis House and I could recognise why. The pipe work had been incorrectly installed and needed relocating to make sure the calorifier heated up correctly to kill off any chance of bacteria forming. More brownie points for Dave.

On a lighter note. We had a rodent problem at Royex House and Pat was struggling to solve it when she was approached by one of the security guards who told her he had the solution.

Enter Eric, the ferret!

Eric's owner was Eric, the security guard. He tells us he will bring in his ferret and let it piss in the riser cupboards and all the mice will run away. He did and the mice left the building in weeks!

The only trouble was Eric (the ferret, not the guard) ate some of the poison and died. We gave Eric (the guard, not the ferret) a job in the mailroom as compensation for losing his best friend.

I needed some help by now and I was asked to recruit a graduate. This was going to be no good to me at all and I told my boss that. Anyway, we interview a few young university types and he eventually agreed that this was not the right option. I needed someone I could rely on and not someone who wanted to pick my brains on maintenance and go off to become a consultant.

So I contacted Andy Steward. Andy, you'll remember, used to have a beer with me at Shearson's in the Lyon Rouge on Friday nights. He was an Electrical Consultant and he and I could make a great team.

I knew he did not know much about the Mechanical side of Building Services and exposed that at his interview so that the firm could see I was not being biased towards him.

When I asked him how the refrigeration cycle worked he said. "A Chiller is a big black box on the roof that produces cold water. What more can you say about it?"

His answer stank but it showed he was not a bullshitter. They loved him and took him on.

Paul Fleetwood joined us next. Paul was a real computer boffin and I needed someone just like him to manage the BMS and computerised fire alarms systems in the new building. I remember impressing upon this young man how high our maintenance expectations were. As he left the interview room, I stood and opened the door for him and the handle came off in my hand. I told him his first job was to repair it.

I now had my own secretary too.

We urgently needed to sort out the maintenance teams I'd inherited. They still seemed to be working as two separate organisations. The new building would need a highly motivated and skilled team and this lot were nowhere near that yet.

We held a meeting at Royex House and I explained the way it was going to be. These lads would all be retrained and everyone would need to take on more responsibilities. We'd need to recruit more Building Services engineers and create two teams with differing skills bases. The higher earning, more skilful and more responsible Building Services team would work 24/7 and a Mon-Fri Handyman team that would take care of the more mundane stuff, like putting up shelves, etc.

This set the cat amongst the pigeons, but it worked and some of the younger guys came forward and said they wanted to be part of the new Building Services team. Some of the older guys wanted to hear about a redundancy package. We recruited a few new guys and also Mike Sullivan their new supervisor from the iconic Lloyds Building. I was ready to take on our new building, now renamed 200 Aldersgate St. Bring it on!

1992
East London Group Training Ltd

*"A charming elderly disabled lady was the last person
I had to make redundant that day, and, when I told
that she was out of a job, she said.
"Oh dear... what shall I do about the money in
the lottery tin?" We all just burst into tears".*

With some of the older guys leaving Clifford Chance's maintenance team, it gave me the opportunity to do something even more unique. It was already unheard for such a large building to be managed by an in-house Building Services team. But I was keen to replace one of the older guys with an Apprentice Electrician. To grow another me, if you like.

So I got in touch with Honeywell Controls who were managing the fire alarm and BMS systems for us and asked them where they recruited theirs. They put me in touch with a registered charity, East London Group Training Ltd (ELGT), and, having shown such a high interest, I was asked to join their management board of Trustees.

We recruited Darren Bacon to the team straight from school in 1992 and I'm proud to say he is still with Clifford Chance in 2007 and is now a team supervisor. Darren was followed another good lad, Nick Humbles, who came out of his time and left us to spread his wings with British Gas. In fact, we have just successfully completed a third apprenticeship with our Liam Kenny coming out of his time and being employed with us as a Building Services Engineer, maintaining our current building.

ELGT, though, were going through a tough time when I joined the board. They had just lost their General Manager who had robbed them of all their cash reserves over time by fiddling the books.

I was the youngest member of the board and, within two years, I was very proud to be elected Chairman of the company.

I really wanted this organisation to work. It was a registered charity and did great work finding work for and monitoring Apprentices' progress in the workplace.

We needed to come up with a plan to stop the financial rot that had set in. Because of changes in Government funding, we were bleeding to death.

Lack of good management was a major problem. They could not afford another manager financially, but, without one, they were going to die anyway in the next two two years.

I took on a new General Manager, Pamela Furness, who really gave it a go and we nearly made it.

Sadly, I could not save them and had to take the final decision to close ELGT as a business. At least, I was able to rely on Clifford Chance's advice to do the right thing at the right time and protect the other unpaid Trustees from prosecution for illegal trading.

I was given the telephone number of an Insolvency Practitioner and met him with Pamela Furness.

He listened patiently to how hard we had tried to save the business and, together, we all came to the decision that there was no other safety plans to execute. ELGT was now formally insolvent.

I was very sad about this and not surprised, but I was taken aback about how fast these things proceed.

"Ok", he says. "You now need to make Pamela here redundant, with immediate effect."

"You will sign this form that I am about to give you and all the assets of ELGT are now frozen. You will not be paying any of your staff a penny in wages and you will need to make all your staff redundant at the office. As of now, you will not spend or indeed earn a penny from your previous activities as ELGT. You will need to close your offices and you are not allowed to remove any goods or materials from your premises.

Once you have signed this document, I will be responsible for all your assets and will liquidate them and draw up a list of Creditors and Debtors and I will decide who will get paid and when. Under the Insolvency Act, the first person to be paid anything from your assets will be this office, which will be handling you affairs from now on. I will be employing your G.M. on a short-term contract until I no longer need her. Any questions?"

I was stunned and just looked at my former employee and shook my head.

I was asked to use a template letter to invite our Creditors and Debtors to an Insolvency hearing and volunteered Clifford Chances premises at which to hold the hearing.

I told Pam that I would deal with the redundancies personally and she said I did not have to, but I felt it was my duty as Chairman, even though I was not paid a penny throughout my time on the board of ELGT.

We left the building and I called Maria to tell her what had happened. I could not speak a word. She just knew instinctively and, in fact, she was able to tell me and I just coughed and spluttered a few words, failing to hold back my emotions.

Pam told me that we had people going on holiday the next day, and that one part time disabled member of staff whose first concern would be what happens to the Lottery money.

I went to the ELGT premises that day, asked the staff to come in one at a time, told then how sorry I was but that they were all being dismissed as of right now and that I could not guarantee they would get paid for this last month. That would be the Insolvency Practitioner's call now.

One guy cut up rough with me. I'm sure they thought I'd run off with the money. In fact, I'd never drawn a penny in expenses. This was a charity I just gave my time to.

I told them all I would be trying to TUPE (Transfer of Undertakings (Protection of Employment) Regulations 2006) as many staff as I could to another training organisation, to keep their jobs in place. But some would have to go. I'd have to also transfer the 100 apprentices we looked after in the workplace to this other organisation.

The charming, elderly disabled lady was the last person I had to make redundant that day and, when I told that she was out of a job, she said. "Oh dear...what shall I do about the money in the lottery tin?"

We all just burst into tears.

I organised a phone call to Inner London Training Ltd (ILT) who were the only other training provider in the area and called them into 200 Aldersgate St. at 8pm the next night. I offered them the future funding we were expecting from over 100 Apprentices that we were looking after if they agreed that night to take four of our staff with them.

I gave them two hours to make their minds up as, the next day, I would be going to the Learning Skills Council (LSC) to tell them we had gone under and I would hand the management of these Apprentices back to them. The LSC would probably hand them onto a College.

The ILT board reluctantly agreed to take on our four staff and we then went to the LSC board to tell them we had gone under, but that the Apprentices' mentoring had been transferred to ILT Ltd.

I am now the Vice Chairman of ILT and our work continues and Clifford Chance and I still proudly host the Annual ILT Apprentice Awards at our London office.

1992–2003
200 Aldersgate St.

"The M.D. of Tuckers, the Mechanical and Electrical Consultants for 200 Aldersgate St took me out for a celebratory lunch at his club. We are talking about the RAC club in Pall Mall, no less. I loved it, and I deserved it, come to that. I was sitting there, taking it all in, when the President of the Club sits down on the very next table. Prince Michael of Kent no less!"

I made a point of visiting the new building throughout its construction and spotted a major flaw in the fit out on level 2. The electricians were installing the lighting conduits too low above the false ceilings making them inaccessible and I wrote an email about it. The project manager (PM) asked my bosses to prevent me from going to site any more, which I was really pissed off about.

I told my bosses that, if I was going to be managing this 500,000 sq ft building, I was not going to inherit a crock of shit; so the PM would have to get on with it and put it right, and make sure the same mistake was not made on the remaining fifteen floors too.

Many years later, the same PM was to tell me that I was absolutely right. I'd just embarrassed them all by spotting something they hadn't.

This particular construction site was a bit of a nightmare to manage because Wimpey, the contractor erecting "the shell and core" (the tower, the lifts, etc), was keen to hand over large parts of the building, and Mowlem, the "fit-out" contractor (office partitions, restaurant, etc) was trying to complete their works and both were at loggerheads with each other.

The Project Management consultancy employed by Clifford Chance was Project Management International (PMI), and Brian Teale and his junior, Andy Driver, led them. They still independently support me in my career to this day.

Brian tells a fabulous story about how he attempted to tell the Partners of Clifford Chance about the difficulties of the contractual relationships on site and how he would need their support to manage the project to a successful conclusion.

Brian was facing them in the boardroom in the Blackfriars House private dining rooms and they are firing questions at him from all sides. These guys are the top legal brains in the world. So he stands up and says. "Guys, Guys... Hang on a minute; I'm on your side!"

While the furore ensues, one of our most senior partners walks away from the meeting-room table and starts to play the piano in the corner of the room. Before you know it, everyone has stopped shouting at Brian and now they are all singing along to the piano.

Brian is standing there with his mouth wide open and the piano-playing partner stops and walks over to him and says. "Brian, I apologise on behalf of my fellow partners. Now, do carry on and tell us how you can get us all out of this mess".

Great story.

Approaching completion in 1992, Clifford Chance decide to take the building from both contractors and set up our own site security management, as this will enable us to get the IT systems into the building and tested in time for the move.

The Developer's team believes we will fail to manage the building and the access they require, but he does know what a great Facilities Management (FM) team Clifford Chance has at their disposal.

Over that weekend, a port-a-cabin is delivered to site, hundreds of keys are handed over, tagged and hung up in key safes. Permit to work sheets are printed up. The power and phones are switched on and we are ready for the 200+ site operatives to arrive on the following Monday.

It's not even 09:30 before the developer's senior guy is on the phone claiming we are causing delays and claiming additional fees. We meet him and his team at the loading bay and show him the set up and he is in awe. He just assumed we could not do it without checking first.

The building is completed and we prepare for the office moves from the nine buildings around the City into our new home. The largest law firm is moving into the largest single-let building in Europe and I'm responsible for all the Building Services and Life Safety systems that will support them in it.

The M.D. of Tuckers, the Mechanical and Electrical Consultants for 200 Aldersgate St, took me out for a celebratory lunch at his club. We are talking about the RAC club in Pall Mall, no less. I loved it, and I deserved it, come to that. I was sitting there, taking it all in, when the President of the Club sits down on the very next table.

Prince Michael of Kent, no less!

I remember thinking how far I'd come from that first day I'd stepped onto a building site aged just 15, over 25 years earlier. I'm now dining with the members of the Royal family!

What my Docker Dad would have made of this, I just don't know.

1992
Moving again

*"I'd stopped the Dee Jaying now. With two young
kids, I couldn't be out all day Saturday leaving
Maria to tend to them. So I hung up my decks,
if that's what old DJ's do".*

Maria and I were living on the East side of the A10, the Great Cambridge
Road, which was more industrialised, with various factories and industrial
estates. Not only were Clifford Chance on the move, but so also were
Maria and I and the girls.

I'd been driving across Enfield each day to the main line train station
at Gordon Hill, and it was clear that the borough had an East and West
divide

The homes on that side of the A10 dual carriageway also reflected it.
There were more terraced houses and council estates and we were living
in a private house on one of those estates.

I was doing far better than I had ever hoped for and I was getting
ambitious, and hinting that I'd like to be the Head of the Services
Department's deputy, but he was having none of it. He recognised that
I was his right hand man, but he did not want to upset the other senior
managers by formerly admitting it. "Just be patient", Keith said, and
looking back, he was right to tell me so.

I now needed to move house. I could afford it and the time was right.
I wanted to be in the better side of Enfield, where the golf courses
were, and Maria and I set about finding a new home. She has always
had recurring dreams about owning a house that never ends, one room
leading to another and another and then another. So we had a shared
ambition in that regard.

We'd extended the house we were living in at Carterhatch Lane, but
the people on the estate were not the type of people I wanted to share
my new life with. I'm no snob, I can't be with my background, but these
people were a bit pikey, and they did not care for their community like we
did in Wapping, and I wanted something better for the girls.

I'd have a tough job selling this ex-council house, as we had a railway line at the bottom of the garden. We didn't care about it when we moved there, but it might bother a new buyer.

So we only took viewings at the weekend when the railway line was quieter, in the hope that no one would even notice it. I even put a clothesline up and would hang sheets out to hide the overhead electric lines, and I used to turn a garden sprinkler on to keep viewers away from the bottom of the garden!

The house was right for first time buyers and they were mainly Greek/Turkish Cypriots wanting to get married and move out from Edmonton to their first home in a better area of Enfield. We were trying to do the same with our third purchase.

The only problem was that these young newlyweds were arriving en masse with all their Aunties, Uncles and Grandparents to advise them on their first purchase.

We got lucky and a young Greek couple put in an offer, which we accepted. I told Maria we would avoid speaking to them until the sale went through, if we could, and make it awkward for them to revisit. Just in case they spotted the railway and pulled out of the sale.

This plan was working until I picked up the phone one day and took a call from one of their fathers.

"Mr David "he says. "I've been looking at the plans and there seems to be a disused railway at the bottom of the garden. Is that true? Does it cause any noise?" I had to think quickly and I say "There is, but have you ever heard any trains go past when you've been here?" "No, of course not" he replies. "Just checking".

They sale went through and we moved to West Enfield and bought a three bedroomed house in a cul-de-sac overlooking a park. I thought we'd finally arrived and had made it.

I thought the house was perfect, and it had a beautiful conservatory too. Maria loved it, but she had plans to increase its size and improve it dramatically.

I was now living in surroundings that were very different from our cold and crowded Riverside Mansions flat in the London Docks.

The first task was to fit a new kitchen. This was no problem for me to do as we had the conservatory just beyond it. So I literally lifted all the kitchen units out and put them in the conservatory and rebuilt the kitchen from scratch in the empty space I'd created.

I'm sitting there in the conservatory having re-plumbed all the washing machines and sinks, etc, temporarily, when suddenly I hear a great gush of water and can't understand where it is coming from. I enter the old kitchen to find it filling with water. Having taken away the old sink unit and pipe work, the main valve had blown off the end of the incoming lead pipe from the street.

This was not down to anything I'd done wrong, but it seems the kitchen unit had been holding the valve in place all these years.

I now have a dilemma. How do I get the valve back onto a lead pipe with full pressure mains water pouring from it? I rush to my tool kit and return to the flooded kitchen. I find the valve in a pond of water that was now forming and ram it back onto the lead pipe and it goes straight on; a quick couple of twists and the locking nut turns and clamps the valve back on. Phew, that flood could have happened overnight or when I'd been at work. So it was lucky it occurred when it did.

The rest of the installation was a piece of cake.

Maria had the bit between her teeth now and we also extended the front of the house to create a new lobby with a downstairs cloakroom in it. This was followed very quickly by a loft conversion to create a 4th bedroom with an en suite bathroom.

This enabled her and me to move upstairs and let the girls have a double bedroom each. We then converted the smallest bedroom into an office den.

Was Maria finished? No way, within 5 years of me installing a new kitchen she got the builders in again and we pulled down the conservatory and extended the house to the rear and went open plan through to the dining room.

Maria made all this happen and I'm glad she did. The additional bathroom at the top of the house and in the porch extension now meant we could knock through the separate bathroom and loo on the 1st floor and create a really nice large family bathroom for the girls to enjoy.

I love this house. But I suspect Maria would like to sell it and do it all over again to another bigger and better house. I think she has a bit of Gypsy in her.

We did miss our two lovely neighbours from Carterhatch Lane.

They were an elderly couple called Kate and Charles. They were in the late 80's at the time. Kate was losing mobility so I rewired the ground floor of their house, so that she did not have to go upstairs to bed.

But, over time, she started to lose her mind to Alzheimer's and wasted away in the geriatric ward in Enfield Chase Hospital.

Sadly Kate had recently passed away after sudden illness.

We'd bring the old boy over for Sunday dinner to our new house. He loved to do a bit of gardening and he taught me so much about it.

His eyesight was failing him though and he kept walking into our glass sliding doors to the patio. One weekend though, he remembered them and checked himself in front of them, he pulled the sliding door across him and then... walked into them. Poor sod, they were already open and he'd just closed them!

I'd stopped the Dee Jaying now. With two young kids, I couldn't be out all day Saturday leaving Maria to tend to them. So I hung up my decks, if that's what old DJ's do.

The Head of the Services Dept. wanted to make a few changes and he made me Facilities Manager. A title I'd been after for over 10 years. I was given the additional responsibility of managing the Cleaning and Security Operations as well as the Building Services in a building of over 500,000 sq ft of prime office space in London. I couldn't think my working life could get any better. But it would.

I was keen to spread my wings even further within the firm and enquired if other offices around the world carried out fit-out works, and, if so, shouldn't we in London (the largest premises) volunteer to help them. I was told that this was not really something I should pursue, as it may not be welcomed. The firm is a partnership and the overseas offices may not want to be seen to be controlled in any way by London. I was also told I had more than enough to do already.

But it was not long before I made my International debut. The Paris office was having problems with their air conditioning.

The building had recently been refitted with a new ventilation and control system. It wasn't working and they were getting a bit hot under the collar, so to speak. The problem was most acute in the meeting rooms.

So I got myself booked onto the Eurostar and went over, taking Kevin Dix, one of my shift engineers, with me.

I quickly found out what the main problem was. The new system was integrated with the windows. A small detector switch would alert the Building Management System computer whenever a window was opened and turn off the cooling to that room on environmental grounds. Nobody had explained the new system to the lawyers.

The French love a cigarette and, of course, whenever they gathered en masse for a meeting, they would all light up and also open all the windows!

The rooms just got warmer and warmer with the cooling isolated. So I was able to point this out to them. I'd made an impact and was delighted.

My French lessons at St Bernard's School weren't entirely wasted after all.

The Clifford Chance Partnership was about to grow even larger. Merging with Punder, a German law firm with offices in Eastern Europe, and with Rodgers and Wells in the U.S.A, we were now the largest Law firm in the World.

1995
Moscow here I come

*"Our excitement turned to concern when we learned
that there had been several terrorist bomb attacks close
to where we were staying. Chechen rebels had attacked
civilian targets in the centre of Moscow,and were
blowing up a number of residential apartment blocks
in other parts of Moscow. I was feeling reasonably
secure as a military guard with a machine gun was now
guarding the Hotel's front entrance!"*

Our Moscow office was also having problems with their air conditioning
and were looking for alternative premises as well.

Clifford Chance were merging with a major Eastern European law firm
to establish Clifford Chance as "Europe's Leading European Law Firm"

The merged businesses had two major office premises in Moscow,
Punder were in one and Clifford Chance in the other.

The managing partner out there asked me to help them to make their
minds up on the short list of premises they had created, so that Punder
and Clifford Chance could then be housed in the one premises in Moscow.

This was an amazing opportunity for me.

So I decided to take Geoff Campbell and Steve Pidgeon, two of our
space planning and moves guys, with me.

We were booked to fly business class from Heathrow to Moscow and
would be met by a "fixer" whose only job was to get us through the chaos
that was Moscow airport at the time.

The flight was fantastic and towards the end we were issued with
landing cards to complete before landing.

These were full of strange questions, like what is your father's first name,
are you carrying guns, and are you carrying drugs?

Like yeah, right, I'm going to answer that my name is Scarface; I have a
machine gun and a suitcase full of heroin!

Geoff had suffered a heart attack a couple of years earlier and was
carrying a large amount of medication. So he puts this down on the
landing card in case the security guards pull him up about the drugs

he is carrying.

We touched down and in no time the cabin doors were opened and there's a guy pointing me out and saying "Mr Exley, please follow me". I was told that someone would meet us at the airport but not that he would actually board the plane itself.

He leads us from the plane past the masses in the airport and bangs on a glass screen to grab the attention of an armed soldier on the other side. He gabbles away in Russian with various references to "....Clifford Chance...David Exley...Clifford Chance".

The glass sliding door opens and we are ushered through and it is closed just as quickly to keep back the masses again. We are led down one of the escalators that had been stopped due to crowds queuing on them.

At the bottom, he calls me close to him. "Give me your passports, please." he whispers. We do, still not knowing who he is. Off he goes. Fifteen minutes later he's back. "Follow me, please". We do, straight past all the crowds in the passport section queue.

He passes all our documents across and the guards examine them. I'm struck by how large the brims on their peak caps are. I suppose they are supposed to make them look scarier. It works.

Their eyes are drawn to Geoff's landing card. "You have drugs!" "Yes" says Geoff. "You have drugs!" he asks again.

There is a crowd of guards around us now. The mysterious guy who met us asks us too. So we show them Geoff's heart attack pills and they relax, thank God. Tell me, who the hell would answer, "yes we have narcotics or guns" on a landing card, if indeed they did. So anyway we're eventually allowed to pass through and out into the fresh air of Moscow City.

"Your limousine is there, my job is finished," says our mystery man, just like a Russian spy. "Were these people all your friends then?" I ask. "Friends... no", he replies. And then he is gone, as quickly and mysteriously as he arrived.

He was employed as a fixer by the travel agency, so that we did not have to wait over three hours to get through the bureaucracy of the airport officials. Presumably, a good few Roubles exchanged hands behind the scenes.

It's clear that we are now in a completely different world to my Wapping. We are whizzed through the Moscow traffic to our first class hotel. The Marriott, no less.

I'm struck by the difference in the architecture of Moscow compared to London and wonder how I can possibly have an impact so far from home and my comfort zone.

The driver tells us we are to change quickly and he will take us to the merger party that is being held at the Punder office.

The hotel is fantastic. The rooms are accessed by walking through long balconies, just like the layout of the flats in Riverside Mansions, but the similarity ends there, believe me. There is a huge atrium below them, and a beautiful young Muscovite woman in a black gown is playing a Steinway piano in the well of the atrium.

We attended the merger party in gardens of the Punder office. Apparently this is where Leonid Brezhnev and Richard Nixon signed a major agreement in 1972. We had a great night and return to the hotel exhausted.

We visited the Punder office the next day to meet with Herman, their Senior Partner, who hailed from Germany.

Geoff already has a nickname for him. Yes, you've guessed it, Herman the German.

He was actually a very charming, handsome, young man and impressed us greatly, although we were taken aback to see him in the meeting room holding a huge pink spatula.

We're discussing property matters when Herman goes very quiet and holds out his hand, palm up, and says, "Shsss"!

He then leaps onto the table and splats a huge bluebottle onto the ceiling with the spatula. We were in fits. A senior lawyer in London would have phoned the Chief Operating Officer and called for an investigation into how such a thing could get into one of our buildings and would have wanted heads to roll, maybe.

The next day we go down to breakfast in the atrium, three East End guys, a long way from home and we are entertained by another musician, another young lady, this time playing a harp.

The lads have a traditional English breakfast but I can't resist trying the Russian caviar on my toast as well.

We visit the various short listed buildings, carry out a space planning comparison, review the services the buildings have to offer and rank the offices.

The lads suggest we give the Moscow Partner a number of options to consider. But my thoughts are that we should just make their minds up for them and tell them straight.

Our views are surprising to them, but we recommend only two buildings be considered. We also chose the Pyanitskaya building over

Kadeshevskaya on space grounds and because the building services there had been completed. We had learned that, in Moscow, you should go with what you see rather than hope to see.

Our excitement turned to concern when we learned that there had been several terrorist bomb attacks close to where we were staying. Chechen rebels had attacked civilian targets in the centre of Moscow, and were blowing up a number of residential apartment blocks in other parts of Moscow. We saw this all on Sky News in the Hotel and phoned home to assure our families we were safe.

I was feeling reasonably secure as a military guard with a machine gun was now guarding the Hotel's front entrance!

I'd managed to inspect the air conditioning systems in the current office building the next day and got to the bottom of that issue and was feeling pretty pleased with myself.

The landlord's engineers were telling me they changed the fresh air filters in the main plant once a week. On inspection, I found they had not been cleaned in perhaps two years.

When we left the office for the hotel that night, the engineers could be seen beating the filters clean in the office car park. By the next morning the Mosenka office was being ventilated for the first time in years and we could literally feel the oppressive atmosphere lift in the office.

All was going well, and we were treated to a guided tour of Red Square and The Kremlin, which was just a short walk from our hotel.

We were all searched as we entered the square. I whispered to Geoff, "Can you believe where you are right now?" A shrill whistle blew and a Red Army guard across the square signalled that talking in the square was not permitted. Another whistle signalled that Steve needed to take his chewing gum out and dispose of it.

We made our way down into Lenin's tomb and suddenly the whole world seemed to stand still for a moment as Lenin's body came into view. There was the great man himself lying proudly in his suit, inside a glass air-conditioned cube.

Back out into the sunlight and we stopped for a moment and stood in front of the coloured turrets of St Basil's Cathedral. I stared up at the Kremlin walls and though back to the days when Joseph Stalin and, later, Khrushchev stood and watched their Red Army troops goose stepping across this famous cobbled square ahead of a variety of nuclear missiles on huge transporter trucks.

Then my mind wandered back to my parents... and what would they say if they could see their boy now. I am suddenly overwhelmed by the grief that they are not here to see this or to even enjoy a phone call from me describing where I am and what I can see. They would have been so proud of my achievements.

We were approached by some street vendors in the square and I bought two large Russian fur hats, an Army cap full of historical cap badges and a very attractive stamp book collection. I also bought some painted Russian dolls and models of St Peters Basilica for the girls.

We flew back to London Heathrow the next day, watching "Four Weddings and a Funeral", starring Hugh Grant, as the in-flight movie. Everyone on the plane was glued to the film but the flight was shorter than expected due to a tail wind and it was interrupted at a crucial moment, right in the middle of a wedding scene in the final minutes of the film.

The plane erupted as everyone tore off their headphones and looked around for a flight attendant to complain to. No point, we were landing and that was it. Or so we thought.

We were taxi-ing back to a stand when the pilot announced that he would take the unusual step off restarting the film just where it had left off so we could all see the end.

He did. There was a collective sigh of relief as Hugh Grant got the girl in the end. Aaahhh!

We got off the plane and collected our suitcases. Unusually, they were all next to each other on the carousel in the baggage hall, and we rushed off to our various cabs home.

I arrived home at 2am feeling very excited and exhausted and was met by Maria and the girls. I threw open my suitcase to reveal the presents I'd bought the family only to find the suitcase was not mine at all. It was identical, but it clearly belonged to a very young Russian woman with a passion for very sexy underwear.

Somewhere in London was a young female tourist with my dirty washing, perhaps!

We did laugh. My clothes turned up three days later.

Clifford Chance was expanding rapidly in London, too, and we now had to move some staff out of 200 Aldersgate St to accommodate more lawyer growth. Our Litigation and Dispute Resolution (L&DR) team were to be moved out to another new development called CityPoint. This proved to be a real pain for them and my team.

CityPoint was a re-furbished 60's building, formerly known as Britannia

House, and had been occupied by Shell. It was in a state of flux when we moved in and the L&DR team spent more time outside the building than in it, as the fire alarms kept going off due to all the building work going on elsewhere in the tower.

Our staff were also locked outside because the lifts failed regularly, and, when they did get in, they were either freezing cold or extremely hot due to faulty air conditioning.

We were just a minor tenant on two floors of this new tower and, unlike 200 Aldersgate St, where we had the full control of the whole building, all I could do was moan about it to our landlord and offer our experience to help him resolve these matters. We were far more experienced than their management team were.

I made a point to remember the problems they faced and vowed that, whenever I got the chance to manage such a large project directly myself again, I'd make sure I did a better job than these guys did.

In 2003 I would get that opportunity.

2000–2003
Canary Wharf

"The London Docks I grew up in was now changing forever. Where once the Canary Wharf Development was just a single 50 storey tower virtually sticking a finger up to the City of London to its West, it was now a thriving business community with over 50,000 office workers in it."

Things were going really well for me now. The family were in good shape and Maria and I were very happy.

Maria's parents had by then retired back home to Ireland and had used their life's savings to sell up and have a new bungalow built, with a bit of land around them. Her Dad had always wanted to breed sheep and train his own sheep dogs and he was very happy to spend every moment he could with them.

My two girls, Kelly and Louise, would spend the whole of their summer holidays at Granny's, tending sheep and riding ponies around their fields.

They became part of the local community in Borristown each year and enjoyed Irish dancing in the local community halls, where everyone came together to enjoy listening to the local bands playing traditional music. They knew every move in all the group dances and loved every minute of their time in Ireland every summer and would cry their eyes out when it came time to come home to England.

In fact, if you were to ask them if they were Irish or English, they would rather not answer for fear of offending anyone English.

Apart from the fact that they were staying in very good accommodation with central heating, I am always struck by the resemblance to my own childhood days, when we went hop picking in the Kent countryside in the 1950's.

Magical times for them and for me.

Back in London, I was given even more responsibilities as my boss started to prepare for his retirement. I was now heading up the Fitness Centre, Health and Safety, Reception, Space Planning, Security and the Cleaning teams, as well as the Building Services team.

The Head of the Dept also took on another Senior Manager, Lee Doyle, to report to him on the "soft services" such as Mail, Printing, Purchasing and Catering.

The London office was continuing to expand and we had staff working outside "the mother ship", 200 Aldersgate St, in other City offices at City Tower, 20 Little Britain, as well as CityPoint.

Senior Partner, Peter Charlton, was getting increasingly concerned that the London office was suffering by being spread across so many locations in the City of London and announced a search for a new London office building to support the whole business, yet again

This was happening less than eight years after we had moved into a 500,000-sqft office.

My team were now working so well that I found myself feeling a little insecure for the first time, which was rather odd.

I had seventy staff, the buildings were under excellent control, and I had more responsibility than I could ever imagine. I should have been sitting back and enjoying the fact that I had cracked it, basically. But there was something inside me that still wanted me to find out if there was still another step or two on this management career ladder I'd clambered onto.

The Head of Dept. was allowing Lee and I the scope to put ourselves into a position whereby he could retire. But that could mean we would have a new boss from outside the firm.

It was finally announced in 2000 that, as there were no premises in the City large enough to house the firm, and none likely to be built in time for our further expansion, Clifford Chance was to leave the City of London and move to the Canary Wharf area.

10 Upper Bank St was identified as our new London office and it could be ready as early as January 2003.

This was fantastic news and took the City and the legal press by storm. I did have some apprehension, as I was not sure whether or not we were going to be the largest tenant of a building managed by Canary Wharf Group, or were taking on the fully repairing lease of the whole building.

I was confident of still having a job one way or the other, but I was really excited at the prospect of managing a major part of a 35 storey, 1,027,248 sqft tower in Canary Wharf that would rival most buildings in Europe and perhaps the World.

I was also starting to feel that perhaps it was time I got myself some form of qualification for the level of management I was operating at.

Remember, on paper, I was still only qualified to be an Electrician.

If I did have to face the employment market again, I'd need something more than the City and Guild's Electricians Certificate Part A and B. Especially if I wanted to continue developing my career in Premises Management.

So I enrolled on a 3-year part time degree course in Facilities Management at Middlesex University. The aim was to get my degree by the time of the firm's relocation to Canary Wharf in mid 2003.

This seemed a good idea in 2000, but it did become pretty stressful after the move to Canary Wharf was announced.

Our staff in the City were not as excited as I was at the prospect of moving to Canary Wharf. In fact, a survey showed that only 34% thought it was a good idea in 2000.

On September 11 2001, that number would shrink even more.

I was just about to attend a meeting with Amanda Burton, the newly appointed Regional Chief Operating Officer, when rumours started to filter through that a small plane appeared to have flown into one of the 110 storey twin towers of the World Trade Centre in New York City.

That changed within minutes to it being, perhaps, a jet airliner.

We had a TV set up in our main library in the building, so I thought I'd pop up there on my way to the meeting and see what all the fuss was about. There was a huge crowd gathered in the library, all watching in total silence. I as watched the screen, not quite believing what I was seeing, a second jet airliner came into view and flew straight into the other tower and everyone in the room screamed in horror.

This was no coincidence, of course, and, as head of security I was already turning my mind to the fact that what was happening in the States could be a prelude to an attack on London.

A simultaneous attack also happened on the Pentagon and a fourth plane crashed somewhere else, presumably en-route to another major target.

I moved quickly up to the meeting room and we all sat there in stunned silence for a few minutes before agreeing to just abandon the agenda and go straight into Crisis Management mode.

Most people in London decided to leave their office buildings and get out of the City entirely and head for relative safety of their homes. Our staff were no different.

Over the next few days, it became clear that this was indeed the work of Al-Qaeda terrorists

Inevitably, our staff became increasingly disturbed that we were moving from a seventeen-storey tower in the City to a major thirty storey tall block on the perimeter of the Canary Wharf development.

The estate has always been seen by the IRA as a legitimate target and was, indeed, bombed by them in 1996 when a major device exploded in South Quay Plaza, killing two members of the public.

Of course, there was very little we, as an organisation, could do to stop such an atrocity at Canary Wharf, but staff were now very conscious about our proximity to the London City Airport. I have to say, seeing the planes zooming in over the towers each time I went to the site gave me a chill down the spine.

Whenever I was asked about what would happen if a plane flew into our new building, I'd just reply, "Most of us would die, but that could happen in the City of London too".

Just to make life even harder, I volunteered to run another London Marathon in 2003.

So let's get this right.... I'll be sitting my finals of a degree course, running 26 miles of the London Marathon, and relocating 3,800 staff of the largest law firm and taking on a brand new 1,027,248 sq.ft. Canary Wharf tower.

Sounds a recipe for disaster, doesn't it?

Well, I would do all those things, and more.

Over the three years from 2000-2003 I worked virtually night and day, seven days a week, on the Canary Wharf project. At the same time, I was still responsible for all the current London office buildings we were in.

In fact, we took another fully repairing lease of a smaller building in the City, 4 Coleman St. This was a 67,000 square foot property that had been fitted out for Slaughter and May, another law firm in the City. This was to be our City office after we moved to the Wharf.

We took it on as there was a concern amongst the partnership that we might lose contact with our City based clients.

This was to be the start of yet another absolutely amazing period for me.

The London Docks area I grew up in was now changing forever. Where once the Canary Wharf development was just a single fifty-storey tower, virtually sticking a finger up to the City of London to its West, it was now a thriving business community with over 50,000 office workers in it.

Transport improvements to the Wharf were approved, and the Jubilee Line extension would soon meet the increased demands being imposed on the Docklands Light Railway.

I was very excited about the move back to the London Docks I grew up in, but also feeling nostalgic about leaving the City of London. After all, I'd worked there since I left school, aged 15, in 1967.

I'd seen so many changes in the City over those 36 years.

When I first arrived, City Gents strode military style from the tube to their offices almost in uniform. Bowler hats set at a jaunty angle, leather briefcase in one hand and a black umbrella in the other. This was carried whether or not it was raining. I swear it was used to measure the length of stride in their steps. There was a familiar "click, two, three.... click, two, three" as it swung beside them, striking the pavement as they marched in unison to work and back to the station/bus stop.

Stockbrokers back then had walked the streets in top hat and tails to get to the Stock Exchange dealing floor. Now, following Big Bang in 1986, young East End wide boys in brightly coloured tabards had moved in and had taken over their patch.

Now there was no need to go into the Stock Exchange at all. It had been deregulated. Computer networks were the way forward now, not the "Old Boy Network"

Swinging umbrellas were replaced by huge mobile phones the size of a house brick. Brown leather briefcases were replaced by black attaché cases. Presumably, the batteries for the phones were kept in them!

Billingsgate fish market had left its home by the Tower of London and had moved to a new huge shed in East India Dock. The old building was now a conference centre.

Covent Garden's fruit market had moved out to Vauxhall, and its market halls had become a tourist attraction with beautiful restaurants and shops.

Fleet Street's newspaper offices and print works had all but disappeared with the changes in technology; the bigger print works and offices had also moved to Docklands.

Smithfield meat market had also shrunk, having fallen under the gaze of the property developers.

While the City of London clung on to many of its institutions and historic buildings, it had changed beyond recognition in so many ways.

It was still my City, though. So, before I left it behind me and moved to Canary Wharf, a business associate sponsored me to be entered for The Freedom of The City of London.

I completed the paperwork and made the application to the Guildhall, which was approved. The Old Boy Network still counts for something, eh? But I'm sure it was my passion for the City and my work within it over so many years that enabled me to achieve the award.

It was such a proud moment when, on 22nd October 2002, I attended the Chamberlains Court in the Guildhall, held the bible in my hand and swore to keep the Queen's peace and to inform her or the Lord Mayor of any plots to overthrow them.

Maria was with me the ceremony and we enjoyed a meal in a local Italian restaurant to celebrate the day.

I was now David Exley, Freeman of the City of London and could now take my sheep over London Bridge without paying any taxes, I could also walk around the City of London with my sword drawn and not be arrested for being drunk in the City!

But I wouldn't be putting any of these benefits to the test, though.

Life at work was getting very busy again for me. I'd go from project meetings at 200 Aldersgate St., to tours of the Canary Wharf construction site to keep an eye on progress. Initially, the site was just a massive hole in the ground.

We'd take the Docklands Light Railway to the site and stand on the elevated station platform at Heron Quays, and look across the whole of Bank St and Upper Bank St and see nothing but an empty space surrounded by a sheet pile wall. This was where the Canary Wharf dock water was being reclaimed and our building was to be constructed.

Within three years, that station would be engulfed by a tower block built over it. There would be seven new major towers, underground shopping malls and public car parks, Jubilee Park, and another 40,000 workers toiling away in some of the world's premier office buildings.

Clifford Chance had the opportunity to create a landmark office fit out of this building, against which other Canary Wharf Group buildings and other Clifford Chance buildings around the world would be judged.

Facilities Managers do not normally get the opportunity to fit out two buildings of the size of 200 Aldersgate St., and 10 Upper Bank St., inside a thirteen year period. I was determined to have a major impact on this new development.

The designs for the new building were to be relatively understated compared to, say, Barclays Bank or Lehmans, but, in themselves, they were still pretty spectacular and it would take us a giant leap forward from 200 Aldersgate St. That was a great building in its day, but it would be thirteen years old by the time we moved and would be by then in need of a major refurbishment and plant replacement.

The new building would be a benchmark facility that would enhance the working lives of all its workforce and clients.

For clients, there would eighty client meeting rooms with dedicated Video Conference Suites, a client hospitality lounge based on the British Airways lounges, a 250 seater auditorium. On level 30, there would be five multi-function rooms and thirteen private dining rooms with spectacular panoramic views over London.

On the same floor, staff would enjoy a 350 seater restaurant with views across the docks, a health club with two squash courts, a 20 metre swimming pool and treatment rooms.

Glazed perimeter offices would allow the natural light and views from this tower to be enjoyed by all staff, no matter what function they undertook.

On level 4, we were building a prayer room, doctor's surgery, a dry cleaners/shoe repairers, and a bar and coffee lounge

This would be "the" place to work and not only make sure we did not lose any staff as a result of the move, but also attract the best young trainee lawyers when they were deciding which law firm to work for.

I ran my ninth London Marathon in April 2003 and looked forward to the results of my degree course in the following months. Later in the year, we would be moving into our new building.

My boss, Keith Toms, had announced that (despite doing a fantastic job with project management of the relocation to Canary Wharf) he was determined that he would not actually relocate there with us, but would retire to Spain with his wife.

I was coming under extreme pressure, but seemed to be coping well, apart from having a slightly elevated blood pressure level.

My GP ordered me to wear a Blood Pressure monitoring device which pumped up and gripped my arm every 30mins and recorded a BP reading. I had to wear it 24 hours a day for 5 days, including overnight.

I was wearing the device on the day I went to Middlesex University to receive the final results of my degree course. I had no idea at all what results to expect and queued up full of anxiety along with all the younger students in the University.

I ran my finger down the list of names posted on the wall. Just as I got to my name, the BP monitor bleeped once and decided it was time to take another reading and the band around my left arm tightened.

It bleeped continuously if the tubes to the armlet were kinked but had only done that once before, when I'd rolled onto them in my sleep.

Two young students standing next to me heard the small air compressor start up and stood back from the list and asked me what was going on. They relaxed when I told them about my blood pressure problems.

I was used to being treated like a freak by the young kids at the University. I'd be stopped in corridors and asked where everything was; they all thought I was a tutor.

My finger was now moving horizontally across the page. I couldn't believe what I was seeing and restarted across the page again. "First Class Honours", it said. I was ecstatic.

My heart skipped a beat I'm sure. It must have done because the BP monitor went into alarm mode and took a second sample to confirm the initial reading!

When I got back to the office, I had a call from Amanda Burton.

I suspected she was going to ruin my day and tell me that I'd be reporting to a newly appointed boss.

I nearly fell off my chair when she told me that she was so impressed with what Lee and I had done over the last couple of years that she was not going to appoint a replacement for Keith Toms, my immediate boss. She was intending to leave things just as they were and allow our Keith's job as Head of Services to just fall away.

So Lee was to become Head of Business Operations and I would become Head of Facilities Management.

I then told her my results from my degree course and how I'd only just got them an hour or two ago. She said, "Well, David, all I can say is that you have had a very good day, haven't you".

It was an incredible day.

I woke that morning Facilities Manager of 200 Aldersgate St and went to bed that night Head of Facilities Management, BSc, 10 Upper Bank St.

I was determined that the new building would be as energy efficient as possible and I met with the Chief Engineer of Canary Wharf Group to discuss how we could best achieve this together.

The main thing I wanted to tackle was the office lighting. The new building would be 1,027,278 square feet across 35 floors. I wanted to improve the quality of the office lighting and have automatic systems that would turn off the lights when the offices were empty. I also wanted to dim them during the day when the building was bathed in sunlight.

I was walking through the City one on my way home and, as usual, I'm keeping a close eye on the new construction sites that are continually springing up in the City.

I was suddenly struck by the view through one of the new buildings. This was a building approaching completion and the lights are on as they are commissioning the fit out.

Illuminating the space is a ceiling full of light fittings of a completely different design. There seems to be twice as many fittings as one would normally see, but they were all relatively smaller too.

I had to get a closer look at these and just walked onto the site and enquired about them and who was managing the building.

The next day, the building manager, who turns out to be an old friend of mine from Broadgate, gave me a tour of the space.

I took the basic design concept back with me to the Canary Wharf project team and said I wanted us to design our own "Shoe Box Lights" for the new building.

This seemed easier said than done.

It turned out that we would have to pay for the change in basic design, a different ceiling throughout and for additional control boxes to all floors because of the change in size and the numbers involved.

But I convinced them that this was worth the effort and the costs.

I was being severely tested at the monthly project budget meetings, as we had to pay a contribution to the developer to have the office lights I'd designed with a company called Future Lighting Designs Ltd.

As they were new to the Wharf, we had to set up a joint venture with them and Phillips to produce and supply the lights I really wanted.

Canary Wharf Group were very keen to meet our environmental aims and, between us, we managed to achieve a BREEAM rating of excellent for the building. The highest energy efficiency rating a modern building could gain.

In fact, 10 Upper Bank St was the first building at Canary Wharf to receive such an accolade and the largest building in Europe to gain that status too.

I was also able to have a major input to the architectural designs and layout of the building including the landlord's areas, such as the entrance hall, lifts and washrooms throughout the building. Something that few tenants ever get a say in.

Over the three years from 2000-2003, I would become a major part of the client design team and the steering group that managed the project.

This meant one day I was in wellies and protective clothing on site checking progress and the next I'd be in major meetings with our senior executives and George Iacobescu of Canary Wharf Group, himself. The full size model of the whole estate surrounded us and we'd be influencing the landlord's designs.

George and Peter had made a verbal agreement that we could have the building specification we wanted "...providing you don't ask for gold taps".

We would pay an elevated rent for 10 Upper Bank St and they would fit the new building out at no additional upfront cost to us. The costs would be recovered from this elevated rent over the life of the lease.

We had to employ our own Architects (Genslers) to design our fit out, the construction of which would then be paid for initially by Canary Wharf Group.

The reality was that the project teams would spend the much of the project arguing over detailed design aspects and whether or not they were the equivalents of "gold taps" or not.

But we got there and the building is a testament to the amazing collaboration between Clifford Chance and Canary Wharf Group. It was quite something to see this green giant of a building rise from a very large pit into the wonderful workplace structure it is today and I am immensely proud to have played such a large part in its creation.

By 2002 Clifford Chance's growth rate in London was so rapid that it was decided that we would take the whole Canary Wharf building on as a fully repairing and insuring lease, and I would manage it and, in effect, become the landlord.

It was about 10% larger than we needed. So it was agreed we would lease 100,000 square feet over four floors back to Canary Wharf Group.

So not only were Canary Wharf Group one of our most highly regarded clients, they were our construction managers, our landlord and now our tenant. This was a very delicate relationship to manage.

As we approached the initial hand over dates I was growing increasingly concerned about the state of readiness. I'd carry out constant checks on the fire alarm system, the fire escapes and the commissioning of the plant. I did now want to inherit the problems that the landlord at CityPoint had.

To maintain the relationship with our client we agreed to take the building on 31/7/2003 without half of our 80 client meeting rooms being available, without the health club or the private dining rooms. That meant they would give me the building to manage and occupy but that we would still have over 350 builders on site trying to complete it.

My main concern was health and safety, security and my being able to manage any serious fire or emergency situation.

It was D-day. Decision Day. It was going to be a very close call as to whether we would take the building on 31/7/2003.

The project team all met on the two floating site accommodation barges, Romulus and Remus, in the Canary Wharf dock basin. Peter Charlton was chairing the meeting and feelings were running high.

Peter asked us all, one at a time, if we thought the building was ready or not. It was my turn to speak. "Don't take it, Peter. It's not ready yet and I'm very concerned. As an FM team we are ready, but, as far as I'm concerned, it is not there just yet," I said.

Some of the project team thought it was, though. So I suspected that they would be advising us to take the building if it ticked the minimum number of boxes it had to from a legal perspective. This was a real dilemma for me.

All the Canary Wharf Group sub-contractors and their suppliers would get a massive pay out triggered by our acceptance of what is called "Practical Completion". This is the time where the occupants, in effect, take full responsibility for the premises and get beneficial use of the property while works continue.

If the building is not handed over it could also trigger claims for additional costs from the sub contractors for delays and perhaps penalty payment demands from Canary Wharf Group against their contractors for lack of completion in line with the programme agreed.

This is a really important moment for thousands of people.

Back at 200 Aldersgate St the first 500 staff had already packed and were living out of boxes in preparation for the largest and shortest migration of office workers in the City of London's commercial district's history.

We adjourned to the site to take a look around the part of the client meeting room facility that would be handed over. It's clear that much has been done to put the space in its best light and it seems odd to be walking around it in the heavy Wellington boots, safety helmets and donkey jackets required for much of the rest of the site.

Peter is staying very quiet.

We make our way onto the escalators that lead down to main entrance hall.

Halfway down, a string quartet strikes up and a group of senior construction guys are standing next to a dressed table with bottles of champagne on ice, glasses and a token golden key in a presentation box on it.

"What are you going to say, Peter," I whisper in his ear. "I'll surprise you," he says with a glint in his eye.

So we get to them bottom of the escalator and Peter walks in the opposite direction to the champagne and asks the construction team to join him on a joint tour of parts of the building.

The string quartet falters and their music stops as we walk off. The leader of Canary Wharf Group's construction team asks me quietly "So what's gonna happen? You guys are taking the building today, right?" "We'll surprise you," I replied, tongue in cheek. I had as much idea as he did.

We eventually find ourselves in the new staff coffee lounge on level 4, which was looking amazing. We unwrapped a few of the new comfy chairs and Peter tells them in his distinctive Geordie accent. "Look, guys, you have done an amazing job, especially in the last three weeks, absolutely amazing...but my team feel that you need a little bit more time to get a lot more done. So I'm going to give you another two weeks...."

You could hear a pin drop and I physically felt the deflation of the Construction team. The relief for me was enormous. I'm ready for the biggest challenge of my career but I needed a fighting chance to be able to take on this new building.

The finishing teams came back into the building that afternoon and the big push was on. We relayed the decision back to 200 Aldersgate St and our staff started unpacking all the documents and equipment they would need for another two weeks in that building.

Two weeks later we agreed to take the new building from our client.

Andy Driver, our in house project manager, and I toured the floors ahead of the first moves, which would now happen in Sept 2003.

The plan was to move 3,800 staff over six weeks and five weekends with a break after the first weekend to just check it bode well for the remaining moves.

It did. The reaction from our staff was amazing. People were just wandering from floor to floor on their first day with their mouths open and saying, "Wow!"

Within months the remaining parts of the building were completed and handed over and staff could really start to enjoy the rest of the building.

The Auditorium was the very last piece in the jigsaw but, sadly, the contractors managed to flood it the night before they handed it over. Somebody left the main sprinkler pipe open ended and, when it came to be filled, it brought the ceiling down. We got it handed over three months later, though.

Keith Toms, my boss, retired and wanted to slip away quietly, but we managed to provide him with a small celebration. He really should have let the firm do something more fitting for all the work he had done, but Keith was a reserved chap and didn't want any fuss made.

I could have sat back now and enjoyed the fruits of my labour but that is not in my makeup.

I was increasingly becoming involved in strategic Property Management issues rather than day-to-day Premises Management now.

Clifford Chance had become a landlord of a major tower at Canary Wharf, and not just a tenant in the City, with serious responsibilities. So, as well as making sure we paid our rent, rates and service charges on time, I now needed to make sure our tenants were doing the same. That was no mean feat to achieve and I carried out a major accounting exercise to establish a reasonable Building Service Charge that could compete with the other towers on the Estate.

These are the costs of cleaning, securing and maintaining the landlord's common parts of the building. I set the service charges at £6.19 per square foot.

Things started to settle down again after the relocation was done and dusted and the building works completed. There was, as expected, a significantly long defects list that Canary Wharf Group and we were working though.

Not a reflection on the quality of their work at all, it just related to the scale of the building.

A year after we moved in the "defects liability period" ended and our ties with Canary Wharf Group's construction team was effectively severed.

2004
Dubai beckons

*A bar waiter approaches us and tells me that a gentleman in
the corner would like us to join him.
He looks very suspicious, not unlike Sidney Greenstreet in
one of those old black and white films starring Humphrey
Bogart. He beckons us over and pats the two spare seats the
waiter has now provided.*

Globally the firm was still expanding. Historically, the London office has always had a direct association with our office in Dubai. So when the time came for them to look for new premises, the Regional Chief Operating Officer, Amanda Burton, asked me to travel out there to help them

This was another fantastic opportunity for me. The business had been established in the original 39 storey World Trade Centre Tower. This, in its day, had been an enviable office location. But now the business district had shifted to the other end of Sheik Sayeed St.

A new major development was underway and we needed to be inside it. The Dubai International Finance Centre (DIFC) was under construction.

This was to be an enterprise zone, much like Canary Wharf had been, and there were financial benefits from being co-located there with some of our existing clients and making contact with some new businesses that were also moving to it.

The development was to consist of six low-rise properties that were to surround an iconic gate-like major building in the centre of the estate. The building would look similar to the tower in La Defense, in Paris, not unlike a staple through which you could pass. Another new building was being planned and visible through the arch of the DIFC building: the tallest building in the world could be viewed, The Burj, Dubai, rising over 146 storeys.

We were already in negotiations with another law firm that was taking most of Building 6. We set to work in London and my space planning team set out the office layout on the CAD system in London.

It didn't look like the right shape of building for the particular needs of a law firm.

My construction projects advisor, Andy Driver, had by now set up his own company, Construction Group Consultancy and had been helping me with the 10 Upper Bank St post completion works. I decided to take him with me, and we flew out to Dubai to view the building. We arrived at the Emirates Air check-in desk at Heathrow to be greeted by two immaculate hostesses in their attractive beige uniforms. They have the hint of a veil too.

I put my suitcase down and handed had over my passport.

The hostess turns to me and says, "I'm pleased to tell you that you and your colleague have been upgraded this evening, sir". I thanked her for that but didn't really understand the implications of it. Andy digs me in the ribs. "Dave, we are already business class. This means we are going First Class".

What an absolutely fantastic experience it was too. We were greeted in our luxurious seats with a glass of the best champagne and a three-course meal to die for. My shoes were removed by a hostess on her knees and a pair of slippers put onto my feet.

We had our own individual TV screens and choices of films and music and then our seats were set to recline into the prone position. The hostess tucked me in and within an hour or so I was away with the fairies until we woke in the morning to a three-course breakfast.

Absolutely incredible and highly recommended!

We arrived in Dubai and were met by a chauffeur in a beautiful and much needed air-conditioned limousine. It was over 40C.

We toured the new building site, which just consisted of concrete slabs for floors, and ceilings and the main lift concrete lift core.

Our fears were correct. The centre core of this building, which housed all the lifts and toilets, etc, was offset from the centre of the floor plate and it meant we could not position lawyer offices around the perimeter and have secretarial work stations outside them as we do in our fit outs.

We could also see that Building 5 was more advanced than Building 6 and arranged a tour of it for the next day.

We adjourned to our 50-storey Hotel for the evening, exhausted. But I wanted to see a bit of Dubai before we flew back the next night and dragged Andy out for a walk down Sheik Sayeed St.

We headed for the nearest bar, but, of course, there were none. There were cafés, outside of which the young people of Dubai would gather to smoke hookah pipes. But drinking alcohol in public is prohibited.

Dubai is an amazing place. It is absolutely spotless, and the buildings are incredibly beautiful and high spec.

We did bump into a couple of Brits who had obviously had a bit too much to drink, which surprised us. We asked them where we could get a drink at this time of night and they told us to go straight ahead to the twin Emirates Towers at the bottom of the road.

One tower forms a residential block, including a hotel and conference suite, and it is attached to its sister tower, which is an office block.

We enter the ground floor and make our way to the lifts and take them to the top floor as directed. When the lifts open we find ourselves in a smoky, cocktail piano bar with fantastic views. This is real East meets West stuff, and various Saudi Princes, local Dubai dignitaries and Western Europeans are enjoying themselves, just as you would in a bar in Canary Wharf.

We buy a couple of Jack Daniels and American Ginger Ales (Jack and Gingers) and stand around looking like a couple of tourists. A bar waiter approaches us and tells me that a gentleman in the corner would like us to join him.

He looks very suspicious, not unlike Sidney Greenstreet, the fat actor who played the shady looking character in a white suit in Casablanca, that marvellous black and white film starring Humphrey Bogart. Anyway, he beckons us over with a gesture of his hand and pats the two spare seats the waiter has now provided.

It turns out he is a journalist with Al-Jazeera, the popular newspaper, TV and news organisation. He also used to live in North London. He could spot English people a mile off and just wanted some English speaking company. He was very entertaining, and even dropped us back to our hotel later that night.

We woke to find it was still over 30 C outside first thing in the morning and returned to The DIFC to view building 5 with Abdullah, who was the guy in charge of the whole DIFC project.

After touring the building, we went to our existing office in Dubai. This confirmed why they needed to move. The entrance to the old World Trade Centre tower was surrounded by ugly concrete blocks to prevent any car bombs getting too close to the Embassies we shared the building with. Security was as heavy in the ground floor entrance hall as it was in Heathrow airport, with scanners and searches being made of everyone who entered.

We met with the Senior Partner and his team and convinced them to take Building 5 over Building 6. It would be a better space fit; we would not be a smaller legal fish in a larger law firm's nest. Building 5 would also be fully occupied by other tenants, unlike building 6, where we and the other law firm looked like being the only two tenants, and most floors would be unoccupied. They agreed with our recommendation.

We went back home that night, but not before we were entertained to a fabulous meal in the open air below the Jumeira Beach Hotel.

On our return Steve Pidgeon set about space planning the Dubai office layouts.

We encouraged the office to follow the designs of the London office, and we managed to create a mini 10 Upper Bank St fit out. We even transferred the new style of office furniture to Dubai.

We were pushing at an open door, though, due to the close link Dubai has with the London office.

The fit out completed, the office moved within a year and grew very successful in the DIFC. Building 6 remained completely empty for over two years, which proved we were right to prevent Clifford Chance from moving into it all along.

I travelled back out to Dubai just after their move and everyone was delighted with their new office.

I was a little concerned about the amount of work that was still going on elsewhere in the tower, though. So I decided to take an unofficial tour of the developer's areas of the tower.

It reminded me of the condition of our Canary Wharf building in the two weeks before we agreed to take it on. Architects and construction managers are always keen to show you their handiwork, but I always look for life safety first. The first problem I found was that the door to the first fire escape I tried was inoperable. Its door handle had been removed to make sure the builders working elsewhere in the building could not access our floor. I had that reinstated ASAP and then walked all the way down the escape stairs to see if they actually led to a place of safety. They did, but the doors to the street were missing, rendering the building insecure.

I needed some reassurance that the fit out of our own area was safe, too, and took a closer look around. The new computer room looked in good condition but I could find no water pressure on the sprinkler system. The same applied to the fire hose reel system. Through an Arab translator, we established that the water had been drained out to prevent any accidental leaks during the construction work. It was reinstated by the end of the day and the building was safe to occupy, and I could sleep nights knowing that was so.

So I left Dubai feeling really pleased with myself and proud to have been able to make such a contribution to an overseas office so far from London. We left for the airport, but not before we spent the night in the comedy club amongst a load of ex-pat lads at The Yacht Club in Dubai. It was a great night and we left Dubai on a high, in more ways than one.

Back in London again, I was starting to feel that life was never going to be the same again for me. I was now having an international impact and had to accept that this was an inevitable path that I was to follow.

The Shanghai office was next on the list of offices looking for some help.

I was starting to think of slicker ways of getting my thoughts on designs and construction across, and, where possible, we used video conferencing technology to hold virtual meeting over the networks.

Andy and I sent some images of Dubai and London out to the office managers in Shanghai who were able to influence the architects out there to adopt a similar approach to our 10 Upper Bank St fit out without us having to go out there.

2004
The return to Moscow

*"We continued through the falling snow and trudging
towards us is a Russian soldier in full uniform.*

*He looks magnificent in his long grey coat, boots and fur
hat. As he approached me, he stops us both and points
up to the old flats behind us and says. "Please, I am only
a poor Moscow soldier. Do you have any change for me
and my family?"*

*There am I thinking how imposing he looks, and that
he would tell me off for giving some money to the poor
woman, and it turns out he is as poor as her.
This really is a city of such contrasts with new building
developments going up all around, but abject poverty
in the same streets".*

Word was starting to spread and I was asked next to take a look at the
plans our Prague office had in place. Their office had recently been flooded.
It was sited in an amazing position, directly on the historic Charles II
Bridge, and was badly affected by the floods that raised the water level of
the river.

They had already picked new premises, Jungmanova Plaza. It was a new
building, away from the riverfront.

This was a brave move and the building was extremely attractive, even
more so compared to the poor specification of their current home. I was
a little concerned how they would make use of the large circular atrium
that formed the main feature of this building.

Steve obtained the CAD drawings for the new building and space-
planned it. Our fears were confirmed. The building footprint was very
small. The office managers were determined to move into this place and
convinced themselves that all they had to do was build smaller office and
buy smaller furniture too!

They had already hired an Architect ("the best in Prague") and were not really interested in what I could bring to the table.

This was frustrating. But my role was to offer "help and assistance" to international offices from London. We are a firm of Partners and it was important that the London office was not seen as imposing itself on the rest of the global offices.

Things went from bad to worse when I saw the actual fit out designs. The client meeting rooms, normally a sober environment, were to have some garish designs. One room had a chocolate ceiling, walls and floor-covering, another, the same in orange and yet another, in red!

I later learned that the architect was well known for her retail work but had not designed an office before. There was no deterring them from the path they were on.

All I could do was voice my concerns and stand back.

The actual fit out lived up (down) to the designs and it reinforced my view that we needed to have some global office fit out standards. We don't have to be like McDonalds and have everything exactly the same in every building, but, surely, we could at least have a common look and feel in them all.

So I took it upon myself to deliver a photographic presentation to our Global Chief Operating Officer, David Childs, so that he could see how the offices were starting to take shape around the world.

Once he saw that London, Dubai and Shanghai now looked similar, he was delighted.

My presentation finished with a request to spend >£10k to produce a Global Office Fit Out Standards Design Document to provide a much-needed steer. I was given the immediate go ahead. But I was advised to change the wording from "Standards" to "Guidelines" to ensure I got cooperation from the partners around the world.

I was delighted and instructed our Architects, Genslers, to turn my thoughts into a working document. Together we produced an invaluable tool that was then circulated worldwide within Clifford Chance.

Apart from the obvious need to have a "common look and feel" or branding of our buildings, it meant that my colleagues around the world did not have to "reinvent the wheel" whenever they moved or renovated their premises.

David Childs decided to take my photographic presentation and show it to all the Global Practice Area leaders. He wanted to emphasise the need for some common practices in any fit-outs around the world.

David and Amanda also produced a detailed questionnaire for our global offices to complete whenever they were considering a major change, expansion or move.

My name was entered into it with an instruction that offices needed to contact me to ensure their works were in accordance with the guidelines I'd produced.

Once I had seen what was being planned, I could encourage the offices to amend their designs and plans and also help them to procure the designers, project managers and contractors to do the work.

The biggest challenge was to get our overseas offices to consider glass-fronted partitions. A huge cultural change. Lawyers are very conservative and traditionally like to work behind closed doors and in solid walled rooms arranged around the perimeter windows of buildings.

These tend to make the support areas closer to the centre of these buildings extremely dark and miserable places to work. These spaces are normally occupied by the secretaries whose job it is to type the thousands of words produced by the lawyers into documents for clients.

I also had the opportunity to influence the choice of furniture for these new office fit outs. Again, this has always been quite a conservative purchase and our new designs took many offices by surprise, as, instead of using traditional slab end desks, we were promoting a fully versatile system-desking solution with movable seating positions, height adjustable tops with integral shelving fixed above them. All desks and chairs were to be the same.

This drew a few gasps, as lawyers and partners outside the UK tend to get larger offices and desks.

I was now busier than ever and had a number of offices, their architects and project managers all e-mailing me daily.

Our senior partner for Eastern Europe, Michael Cuthbert, rang to tell me that he was planning to move the Moscow office and that he would be looking to me to help with the designs.

Basically he was telling me "I want you to install the same fit out you have in London".

We talked about my previous visit and how we had selected a building for them to move to. Michael explained that it was very helpful and they secured additional space in the existing building at a knock down rate and the landlord fitted out a new floor for them and improved his management.

However, a recent fire in the premises was the last straw for them. Smoke had made its way through the building without any fire alarms working and, when his staff self evacuated, they found the final fire exit doors padlocked. Luckily, no one was injured or, even worse, died as a result of the fire. But they had now had enough of Mosenka and that particular landlord.

We acquired CAD drawings from the developer and set about trying to design the new Moscow office.

The new building had a similar layout to our London office tower at Canary Wharf. The main concrete core of the building, which houses the lifts, toilets and stairs, was set directly in the middle of the structure.

Steve laid out the offices and client reception and meeting rooms and we were to take these initial plans with us to Moscow.

Steve was getting excellent at this now. You can never appreciate how best to design a space layout until you see the orientation of a building and most importantly the views from the windows!

I was up for this challenge and Andy and I packed our overnight bags again and we were to be on our way to Moscow in a matter of weeks.

Russian law dictates that you need a visa to enter Russia, so this was arranged. We travelled on tourist visas as we only planned to be there for a few days.

I'd been to Moscow previously but I was still very excited about going back.

We flew Business Class from Heathrow and were able to use the Business Lounge.

We were ushered through the Executive check-in area and security checks and entered the shopping mall. Andy had travelled in this way before but I was like a novice, really.

He knew his way to the Executive Lounge and we were met by a smiley bevy of hostesses who checked our tickets and allowed us through.

Andy flashed a BA card at the hostesses and they rearranged our seats on the plane so that we were sat next to each other and I got the window seat, which I prefer.

We placed our flight bags and coats with the concierge and picked up a newspaper or two and settled into our comfy sofas.

This was far more civilised than tourist class, I can tell you.

After a complimentary cappuccino or two, we took our complimentary breakfast from the buffet area. I had smoked salmon, as I recall.

We knocked out a few emails on our BlackBerries and Laptops and talked about who we would want to meet in Moscow and relaxed some more. No need to worry about flight times and departure gates while you are in the lounge, as the lounge hostesses broadcast these at the right time.

It was getting nearer to midday so we ambled up to the bar for a couple of Jack and Gingers on ice. Complimentary, of course.

Before long it was time to board the plane and enjoy the comforts of in-flight business travel. A light three course meal, an in flight film and a few drinks on the way.

A flight attendant asked if I was a frequent flyer or not. I told her I was new to this lifestyle but that I did expect to travel widely over the next year. She gave me an application form to join the British Airways Executive Club. I'd start at blue card level. This would enable me to earn air miles for business trips and hotel stays and possibly move up to silver and maybe even gold card level where the rewards are even higher.

I thought to myself, this is the life!

I stared out of the window as the sun was setting and again got quite emotional. Me way up here, my family down below me, and my thoughts turned again to my parents and the life they had led. What they hell would they think if they could see me now? They would be over the moon for me.

We arrived in Moscow and much had changed since my previous visit seven years ago. We had landed in Sheremycheva airport and it now seemed much more organised than my trips before. We did not need a fixer to get us through the airport as before.

The bureaucracy was still there, though, and we had to stand in long queues while miserable looking security cards took an age to examine and approve our entrance into Russia. I swear they have an egg timer behind that screen and only allow you through once 10 minutes have elapsed!

That ordeal over, we were now in the arrivals lounge and, after fighting our way through all the taxi touts, we found our driver Yuri, as expected.

"Dobrodin, Yuri", I exclaim. "Dobrodin", he replies, with a slightly bewildered look on his face. I'd been practicing my Russian accent and how to say "Good Morning" for days.

It freezing cold and all the cars in the car park are filthy. There is so much anti freeze spread on the streets that there is little point in washing them every day.

Our jeep was spotless. I'm sure this is because Michael Cuthbert would expect nothing less for his clients and partners. Michael has his own fleet of cars and drivers to cope with Moscow's notorious traffic jams.

We speed through the outskirts of the city and arrive at our hotel. The Hyatt. One of the best in Moscow.

We showered and arranged to meet at the bar. Michael is coming over to discuss the plans for the next day or so. We all go to the bar at the top of the hotel and take in the view over the rooftops to the Opera House, the Seven Sisters (a group of historic towers) and the Kremlin, which is with walking distance.

Another partner, Marc Bartholomy, joins us. The plan for tomorrow is to visit the existing office at Mosenka and then to meet Hines, an American developer, who is constructing a new office tower called Ducat III in Gasheka St.

Michael tells us this will be the best building in Moscow and we need to move quickly to secure space within it.

We were pretty knackered by now as Moscow is 4 hours in front of London and it was a four and half hour flight. So we call it a night.

The next day we enjoy a full breakfast and head off in one of Michael's jeeps to the existing office.

The building was very familiar to me and, once inside our demise, I was immediately struck by how dingy and dark the place was. Mosenka was once the place to be but, compared to London, it was awful. The secretarial bays had no access to any daylight or any views through the windows, as the perimeter offices obstructed these with solid fronts on them.

I just knew the staff would love the designs I had in mind for them. Having said that, the lawyers in their perimeter office might resist the glass fronts I'd be proposing. They did in London and Dubai so why would they be any different in Moscow?

Having taken a look around and met Fargane Aljoshina and Pavel Bulgakov, the office and IT managers, we headed off for the site of the new Moscow office.

As we approached the new building, it started to dawn on me that this project was going to be a real challenge. The tower was still being erected!

There is a big difference in fitting out a floor or two in a property that has been in existence for some time and a building that isn't actually there yet!

We were met by a group of the developer's project managers at the base of the building and taken through to what would eventually become the entrance lobby, and then to a stairwell that would form a fire escape one day.

We walked the fifteen or so flights of unfinished concrete stairs to level 7, one of the floors we would be taking.

I was amazed to see so many women working on the site. You would never see that in the UK at all. These ladies were cementing the walls of the staircases while precariously balanced on what may just about be described as a scaffold. The ladies themselves have made these scaffolds from odd bits of timber found on the site and there was no handrail in sight!

It was -25c on site and there were no windows anyway as yet. So the cement they were using was freezing before they could get it onto the walls. I couldn't for the life of me see how anyone could make any progress in this weather at all.

But I was told this was Moscow and not London and that they were used to working in these conditions.

Once I'd got my breath back we started to take in the views from the building at this level. Comparing these to the space layout that Steve had produced, I was able to orientate myself.

We were now standing in the area we'd allocated to the client reception and meeting rooms. I glanced out of the building and asked what the dilapidated old factory building below us was used for.

"That place"? "Oh, that is the Embalmers," said one of the Russian Project Managers without a shred of concern.

So we had our first change of layout already!

Walking to the opposite end of the floor, I could spot a number of the Seven Sisters on the horizon. Sadly, no sign of The Kremlin buildings, though. We needed to be several floors higher to get any view of it.

So all we had to do was flip our space plans and our clients could enjoy the best views from the building, instead of us hosting business lunches overlooking the undertaker's yard!

We adjourned to the developer's offices, which were just over the road from the site, and enjoyed a hot coffee to warm us up again.

We were entertained to some graphic images of how the building would look when completed. While it would not look out of place in Central London, it would be a fairly spectacular building for Moscow.

By now, though, Andy and I were coming to the same conclusion. We needed to pass the contract risk of fitting-out back to the Developer, if we could. The risk was that we could end up not getting access to the building for some time during its construction. Delays would not be in our control. In this way, we could even, perhaps, complete the horizontal fit-out ahead of all the landlords' services being completed or commissioned.

In essence, we could have a completed office fit-out, but no air conditioning as the rooftop chillers might not be in place. A great office, but maybe we would not be able get to it, as the lifts might not have been finished.

The partners, Michael and Marc, both listened to our concerns about the program delivery problems we could foresee, and agreed we should employ Hines, the developers, as our construction manager.

We felt really good about that.

Andy and I went back to the hotel and changed and went out for a drink. The snow was about 6ft deep in places, above the parked cars, in fact.

We found a local bar and took in the freezing cold atmosphere of Moscow at night.

We are trudging through the driving snow on our way back to the hotel, when I hear a call behind me.

When I look back, there, on the pavement, is a Muscovite woman with a very old horse on a rope. She puts her hand out and pleads, "Please, please, I am only a poor Moscow woman who cannot feed her horse, do you have any spare roubles, please?"

I was so stunned I gave her a few roubles and she wished me luck. We continued through the falling snow and trudging towards us is a Russian soldier in full uniform.

He looks magnificent in his long grey coat, boots and fur hat. As he approached me, he stops us both and points up to the old flats behind us and says. "Please, I am only a poor Moscow soldier. Do you have any change for me and my family?"

There am I thinking how imposing he looks, and that he would tell me off for giving some money to the poor woman, and it turns out he is as poor as her. This really is a City of such contrasts with new building developments going up all around but abject poverty in the same streets.

He got some roubles, too.

Back in the hotel bar, we have one more drink before going to bed.

The bar is now full of high class prostitutes and Andy and I have a giggle at all the old western men walking to the lifts with these very young girls, desperately trying to pass them off to reception as their nieces, no doubt.

Unfortunately, Andy had dropped his mobile phone in the snow-filled street the night before we left. He never heard it hit the ground, of course, as it landed in the deep, pure white snow on the pavement. He was lost without it.

So Andy Driver and I were out in Moscow for what we believed would be the final trip we would make there. The furniture was arriving and being installed across the two new floors in the Gasheka St building.

It's Friday night and Michael Cuthbert, the senior partner for the region, is in London for a function, and all his office staff are packed and ready to move that weekend.

Andy and I had come just to sign off the building works but we got our jeans on and started to muck in with the various teams. I spotted a problem. All the plugs on the mains leads that would feed each desk were the wrong type and didn't fit the international sockets that were in the floor void.

This was a potential disaster and we couldn't get the 150 plugs we need in Moscow for this weekend.

So I rang our maintenance supervisor in London and pleaded with him to get a suitcase full of them and give them to Michael and tell him to bring them back to Moscow in the morning.

Anyway, Michael arrived the next day with the plugs and 150 matching sockets too.

"There you go, Exley" he says proudly.

I took one look at them and I could see they were the wrong type.

But, never mind, we now had plugs and sockets that matched, I just had to tell the Russian Electricians to spend all Saturday and Sunday changing them on all the desks and in the floor void.

Just imagine it. Me making male and female finger gestures to simulate sex and holding up the new male and female plugs and sockets to the Russians. "You put all so, da?"

We managed to get the power sorted without telling Michael how close he came to having the office out of action for a week.

My main concern, though, was getting the fire alarm system finished off, and commissioned and made live before the staff moved into this new building. I also managed to get the fire suppression sprinkler system livened up that night.

My persistence with the contractor paid off and I went to bed a happy man.

Moscow opened on time and everyone was happy and we went to their office party.

Just a couple of months later, I would take a call at home on Good Friday telling me the Moscow office had been evacuated due to a fire. Flames were running up the outside of the building.

We exercised our Business Continuity Plan (BCP) and I took part in a number of voice conference calls across our global network that weekend.

The staff were moved out to Allianz, one of Michael's client's, who luckily had some vacant premises.

Andy and I went back out to Moscow and walked through the power-less premises and up the ten floors to our space.

The landlord showed us where the sprinklers on our floors had put out the fire in the landlords exterior lighting system that had been the source of the fire.

The flooding of the floors by the sprinkler system had protected the building from falling down but had flooded all the floors below, and filled the basement switch rooms with water, taking out the power supplies for the next few months.

I tapped myself on the shoulder for getting the life safety system progressed to completion against the odds before we left in January.

While we were there, I carried out a risk assessment of the temporary accommodation we had moved into and got any defects sorted before I left again for London.

Three months later, the Moscow office returned to a refurbished office in Gasheka St.

I was continuing to build on my reputation and was invited to the Warsaw office to assist them with their office expansion too. Nick Fletcher, our senior partner in Warsaw, was very appreciative the help Andy and I were able to provide.

They, too, had employed another local architect. She had her view on how a Law firm should look and it was hard going initially to overcome her resistance and those of the Polish partners of the original firm Clifford Chance had earlier merged with. But, by the end of the two days, we were there, diplomacy won out and we compromised on the designs a little.

The Polish partners were delighted to be "meeting the London guidelines" and getting the "London look".

By now, I was upgraded to a Silver Card British Airways frequent flyer card due to air miles I was clocking up.

So I could access any of their VIP lounges, pick my own seat and get preference on busy flights.

Over the next few months, I was also invited to give the Paris office's Disaster Recovery (DR) IT centre the London approval. Barry Shambrook of Tucker Consultancy, our Mechanical and Electrical advisors, and I went over to see it for the day and flew out from the London City airport, close to Canary Wharf.

We detected a single point of failure in the power supply system, which surprised us as it was a very expensive site provided by a DR Service provider that specialises in such installations.

Six months after we reported on that, the electrical system went down.

This was disappointing, but Barry and I were then asked to inspect the DR centres in Frankfurt, Amsterdam, New York and Washington.

Our findings formed a major report, which has generated a rethink on the Mechanical, and Electrical service provisions around our global IT facilities network.

2005
My last London Marathon

*I dig deep along The Embankment with my eyes fixed
on the blue line painted along the length of the course,
refusing water now, as it will not benefit me any longer.*

In 2005 I ran what I'm sure will be my 10th and last London Marathon.

I needed to do this one for a number of very good reasons. Billy Jones, the guv'nor of The Three Swedish Crowns pub in Wapping, and a very good friend, had died in the winter and I wanted to do something for his family and friends.

I also thought that nine was an odd number to leave my marathon experiences on. I may as well have finished after 6 or 7 say. 10 had a certain ring to it, double figures, etc.

At 53 years old, I'd also just become older than my Dad had been at his death. This had been playing on my mind and I was starting to get concerned that perhaps my own life was perhaps coming to a close. I wasn't ancient yet but this kept nagging away at me.

Looking back, it seems so strange that I had managed to do so many of these marathons since my first in 1989. You have to remember that I was 37 years old then and was not in great shape. I liked a beer or two, my usual weight was 15 ½ stone and I had torn a cruciate ligament and lost cartilage in my left knee, which had left me with muscle wastage and a weakened left leg.

I'd run each of my previous 9 marathons as if it was my last and did not keep fit in between each race.

I loved the event, though, and I know I have inspired others to take it on. Let's face it; if I could do it, anyone could, really.

I must have raised over £30,000 for charity, mainly the Cancer Macmillan Fund that provides care for the terminally ill and supports their families throughout that care.

So I set out my training plan again and got myself fit and lean enough to haul my old body around the 26.2 mile course for one last time.

I'd bombarded Bill's friends and family with emails and hoped to have a good crowd cheering me on. Those who replied told me that they would be at the City Pride pub on the Isle of Dogs in East London.

Having trained all winter, I arrived at the Greenwich start in a relative heat wave for any given Spring. I knew I was going to struggle this time. I was older, less fit, and there would be no shade for most of the worse part of the race.

I was dressed as Superman again, but ,this time, I had a lovely photograph of Billy and the words "For Billy" on my back.

I was doing quite well and just thought I'd enjoy the day and aim to just get round really and not put any time pressure on myself. The days when I could finish in less than four hours were now behind me.

I was approaching Tower Bridge that has always been a significant and emotional point for me. Once I was over the bridge, I knew I was half way round. It also meant I'd be seeing my family and running through my manor, Wapping, where I grew up.

I always felt frustrated each year as I ran over Tower Bridge as Bob Wilson, Sue Barker, or any of the TV celebrities on the bridge had never called me over for an interview.

This year was my last time and it was so special with Bill dying. I managed to catch the eye of one of the TV crew whose job it was to spot lunatics in fancy dress like me.

"Hey, mate, give me a break, will you? It's my 10th and last one, and I'm doing it for my mate who died", I called out to him.

It worked. As I approached the centre of the bridge in the middle of a mass of runners, there's former Olympic champion, Sally Gunnell, with a radio mike in one hand and the other waving frantically at me.

So I acknowledge her and walk over to her trying to gather my thoughts on what I might say. She's very kind and I blurt out that it's my 10th and last race and spin around to show the camera Billy's picture and declare the day is all about Bill and his family. Not really knowing if anyone is seeing any of this at all.

I then ran on with a cheery wave, feeling uplifted. Half a mile later I hugged and kissed my family on The Highway.

A few more miles and I'm passing The City Pride frantically looking for Bill's family, but there is no one there and my tears of joys turn to tears of desperation.

The Isle of Dogs can be one of the longest sections of the race for me, so I decide to grit my teeth, dig deep and get on with it.

I was a little disorientated coming off the Island and feeling low when, suddenly, a huge cheer goes up. I bring my head up and there they all are.

Billy's family did turn out after all. The race passes the pub to the front and the rear, and they had their 20-30 seats at the rear.

What a fantastic feeling that was. I spun around again and showed Bill's picture and we all ended up in tears.

"We just saw you on the telly, Dave. Thanks so much, Dave. Keep going, keep going," they shouted. I was elated for them and I was floating on air for the next mile or so as the race turned back on to The Highway again for the return leg back through the City and onto the finish at The Mall.

Nothing could stop me from finishing now. I dig deep along The Embankment with my eyes fixed on the blue line painted along the length of the course, refusing water now, as it will not benefit me anymore.

Turning into The Mall, I spot the finish line. The digital clock says it's taken me longer than any previous time, but who cares.

I break into a real sprint to the finish and pick up my 10th and last ever London Marathon medal. No one can take that away from me now. And I have every right to feel as proud as I do.

2006
New York, New York!

"Is this where it happened?" I asked nervously. Half
expecting him to say something crass, like "Where what
happened?" But no, he was very courteous and pointed into
the open hallway entrance to this fairly anonymous building
behind his back and said. "Right there, Sir....Right there". The
hairs on the back of my neck stood up.
I was standing on the very spot that John died.

During 2006, Grace McLaughlin, the Office Manager in New York, invited me across to help her with her Disaster Recovery process plans.

The landlord in New York (NY) closes the building down entirely for a weekend each year to carry out major maintenance to the building systems. So the firm switches its IT provision to our Washington (DC) data centre.

So again I took Barry Shambrook of Tuckers with me so that we could add our thoughts on the systems in the NY and DC data centres to the growing review of our IT provisions around the world.

The report was taken on board and the firm is currently looking to move those data centres to an even higher spec service outside of the offices themselves.

I also took my Business Continuity Manager, Sam Clark, with me.

He and I stayed over the weekend of the power down while Barry flew back home.

Work aside, I was thrilled to be in the States for the first time in my life and took the opportunity to visit the White House and the Lincoln Memorial in Washington

You see these places on the news over the years, JFK, Nixon, etc, in the White House and you can't help being moved at the aura of Lincoln sitting in his chair at the famous memorial.

I stood in the same spot where Martin Luther King made his "I have a dream..." speech and was moved to tears.

Sam and I flew up from Washington the next day to the Big Apple.

New York was everything I hoped it would be. The landlord did what he had to and our IT colleagues recovered the systems ok and we went out for the night to the Italian sector in Little Italy for a celebratory pasta meal with Big Tony, the IT director.

We arrive at the restaurant and he points out where a local Italian mafia guy had been shot dead. I naively ask if that was in the 1930's, but "No", says Tony "last week!"

Shit!

I was determined to make the best of being in the Big Apple, so we stayed the weekend and set off for the Statue of Liberty. This meant taking a metro journey out to the harbour and picking up one of the many ferries.

We were thoroughly searched before joining the queue for the boat. You get a really good perspective of the city from the boat and you are reminded of the recent events of 9/11 by the missing twin towers and the fact that the ferry was escorted most of the way by a navy gunboat.

The Statue of Liberty is an amazing sight and I was surprised to find it a bright green having previously thought it to be made of stone. It's copper, of course, and now covered in verdigris.

You can't help but put yourself in the shoes of the millions of immigrants who have approached America through this route.

On the way back, we decide what we will do for the rest of the day. We both agree we must visit Ground Zero, the site of the fallen World Trade Centre twins towers brought to the ground after two fully laden passengers jet airliners, United Airlines flight 175 and American Airlines flight 11, were flown into them by Al Qaeda terrorists in 2001.

The site is a short walk from the harbour.

Sam and I just stood in silence, staring into the huge pit that is now a place of homage for so many Americans.

2,998 people died in this tragedy and it felt strange to be actually standing there.

It seemed even odder to find street traders selling books and photos of the event, but I bought some to take home anyway.

As we walked away, we stood and paid our respects at a bronze memorial set into a wall that recorded the names of all the fire fighters who lost their lives that fateful day.

Just a turning away, we came across a tiny fire station with two fire engines in it. There was little space for anything else. I stood and looked up at the sky above the fire station and just tried to imagine what those guys felt as they looked out of that tiny fire station at the scenes above them that day.

Again my emotions got the better of me.

Sam wanted a drink. We eventually stumbled across a bar about half a mile away from Ground Zero. It was as if the area had been sanitised of hard liquor stores, etc.

I wasn't sure about this place. It looked like a gay cowboy bar from the outside. We went in. Anything for a laugh by then.

Two young waitresses in miniskirts and cowboy boots were entertaining everyone behind the bar. Sam and I pulled up a couple of stools and ordered some beer and, yes, they slid them down the metal bar surface towards us.

We were enjoying the atmosphere that the Rock & Roll jukebox was providing when suddenly the two waitresses leapt onto the bar counter and started an impromptu dance right above us.

Guys were tucking dollar bills into their boots to keep them going.

It could only happen in New York, eh?

We made our excuses and left.

Sam wanted to pick up jeans for a family member and as I can't stand shopping, I decided to head for the Dakota Building where Mark Chapman had shot John Lennon on 8th December 1980.

I took a subway train down to Central Park and sat there humming "How deep is your love" by the Bee Gees, remembering the journey John Travolta made in the film Saturday Night Fever.

A crowd of middle-aged black men boarded the train and made me a little nervous. But then they broke into a barber quartet style song and entertained the carriage. They were buskers and very good too.

I left the heat of the platforms and walked up the main road that runs alongside Central Park. There's no sign directing you to the Dakota Building.

There are a few people like me wandering around aimlessly. I noticed a young person taking a photo of a building for no apparent reason and I approached the doorman.

He seemed to connect with me straight away.

"Is this where it happened?" I asked nervously. Half expecting him to say something crass, like "Where what happened?" But, instead, he was very courteous and pointed into the open hallway entrance to this fairly anonymous building behind his back and said. "Right there, Sir... Right there".

The hairs on the back of my neck stood up. I was standing on the very spot that John died.

I wanted to stay around but it felt strange to do so as there was nothing to celebrate, and I'm sure the residents did not want a constant reminder of that event.

So I made my way across the road to Central Park, as I wanted to find the Strawberry Fields memorial place. Again, there was little signage, but I became aware of a number of people wandering off in the same direction.

Just a few hundred yards into the park and I was there. There isn't much to see, really. Just a circular paved area where three paths meet .The words "IMAGINE" have been set into the stonework on the ground.

There were quite a few people milling around, all not knowing what to do or say. People from every part of the world. All here for the same, united reason. Some sad, some happy, most just reflective, like me.

Benches surround the circular paved area. One bench became free and I went and sat on it just to take in the atmosphere, and, yes, there was a lot of love in the air that day.

I became aware of a couple of musicians unpacking their guitars across the area. One lady has a violin, another totally unconnected person has a tambourine.

Before long guitars break into the opening riff on "Yesterday" and, as a group, we all join in singing. It was extremely moving and I called Maria on my mobile to share the moment with her.

New York is full of contradictions and one of the most exciting places on earth.

They are so patriotic, too. It's an amazing place.

2006
We were there!

"It was a really emotional thing to do and I loved every minute of it. I seemed to have narrated most of the film clips on the TV program".

Its 2006, now, and the 40th anniversary of England's 1966 World Cup victory over West Germany is approaching. So I set about trying to buy a replica red football shirt on the Internet, to wear for fun.

While searching the various websites, I come across a BBC website asking fans to record their memories of that great day. Most of these are of watching it on T.V.

So I write to tell them of my experience of being at the game. I then get a call from the BBC who want me to appear in a BBC TV programme called "We Were There!" The program would be broadcast on the anniversary itself.

Jackie Charlton and Henry Cooper were on it too, along with one of the blokes that ran on the pitch at the end. It was a really emotional thing to do and I loved every minute of it. I seemed to have narrated most of the film clips on the TV program.

I was interviewed on camera in front of Riverside Mansions in Wapping.

The BBC sent me my own copy as a keepsake.

Whenever I need a little cheering up, I get that DVD out and play it again, and can go back again to that wonderful time in 1966.

My friend and former pro boxer, Jimmy Flint, had appeared on BBC's Grandstand, a midweek sports program, many times at the end of the 1970's.

As the BBC producer was delighted with my contribution to the World Cup program, I rang and asked him to do me a favour.

I asked him if the BBC had kept any of Jimmy's fights in their archives, and would they let me have anything they had.

Jackpot! Three days later, my man came back to me to tell me that he had five of Jimmy's fights, all of which were knock out wins, too.

I rang Jimmy to tell him that I had managed to get these and that I wanted to organise a night out in a Wapping pub so that he and all our old pals can relive his fights from 1978-80 as we'd never seen them from that day to this.

Jimmy then tells me that a film is being made about his ill fated boxing and acting career and that the film crew was keen to come along and record the event for the film.

So I get all my old mates and the film crew to agree on a date and book The Old Star in Wapping for the event. I leave work a little early that Friday night and make my way to Wapping.

When I open the door I'm blown away. It was like being back in the 70's again. The place is packed with our mates and their sons. A large group of young men have stayed behind having finished their football matches in the new Wapping Sports Centre, and The London Ex Boxers Association is there, too. Former Heavyweight Champion, Billy Aird, is holding fort in the bar and Steven Berkoff, one of Jimmy's new actor friends, has also come to see the fights.

The film crew is relieved to see me, as they have been setting up lights and camera positions all day.

I put on the "We were there!" 1966 World Cup film I'd appeared in to entertain the crowd while I was busy doing an interview piece to camera in a corner of the pub. This interview will appear in the film, should it ever get published, that is.

We had a few beers, and, after the grub appeared, I grabbed a microphone and called the pub to order and explained what everyone was about to see. The film clips were short, as indeed were many of Jimmy's fights. So I'd done a bit of editing and cut in some sections in between the actual fights, where I described where the fight was taking place and the date, etc, to pad it out.

Suddenly, all the film crew's lights came up and they followed Jimmy and I around the bar, focusing tight on Jimmy's face as he watched himself fighting again.

The pub went crazy as we watched Jimmy knock his opponents out again for the first time in nearly 30 years.

It was a fantastic night and Jimmy was delighted. I gave him his own personal copy on DVD and Video.

Jimmy also got his one man show into the theatre again towards the end of 2008, at Wilton's Music Hall, a genuine music hall in Wapping that is being renovated. His performance was also recorded by the film crew for the movie that we all hope will re-launch his faltering acting career. I'm really looking forward to that, especially for Jim.

Jimmy's acting career started in a local play called "The third and final round" at the Half Moon theatre in Mile End, with Johnny Bardon, who now stars and Jim Branning in BBC TV's East Enders.

Jimmy has appeared in TV shows such as Casualty, Kavannah Q.C., with the late John Thaw, and films such as "Lock stop and Two Smoking Barrels" with former Wimbledon FC footballer Vinnie Jones, as well as being in "The Krays" with former Spandau Ballet pop stars, Martin and Gary Kemp, who played the lead parts.

My career continues to reach almost dizzy heights for me, and Jimmy has had two very public failed careers behind him in the ring and on stage and screen, which seems very unfair to me.

2008
Broad St Boxing Club

"I felt a little ashamed that we had such a fantastic sports facility in our Canary Wharf office, where lawyers can play squash, swim and exercise for free, and these poor kids were paying weekly subs (subscriptions) to train in awful conditions".

I still go back to Wapping on a regular basis, but I now have to send a round robin email or text to get everyone together for a few beers, whereas, years ago, I'd just call up at my pal's flats from the street.

During the writing of this book, I took one of many journeys back to Wapping only to find the local underground station closed, forcing me to cut my journey short and leave the tube network at Shadwell. Transport for London is upgrading the East London line to link Hackney in North London to the countryside of the South East.

In the short distance between Shadwell and Wapping I found myself again passing the building where I trained as a young boxer. The building was boarded up at ground floor level and looked abandoned.

But I could hear the sound of someone pounding a heavy bag and looking up to where the gym used to be, I could see a light or two on and the shadow of a boxer against the filthy windows.

I couldn't believe what I was seeing. Could the club I boxed for in 1965 still be in existence? I had to go in and find out.

I climbed the unlit stairwell to the 2nd floor and walked in. The place fell silent and everyone stared at me. They must have thought this stranger in his business suit, shirt and tie to be a copper, maybe.

The place looked locked in a time warp. Everything looked exactly the same as I left it 43 years ago. Even the boxing ring that my Dad and his dock mates put together was still there.

I spotted Johnny Gleed, the trainer who took over the management of the club just after I stopped boxing all those years ago. He has been up there, unpaid and working with young men ever since. A guy named Terry Henry assists him.

I re-introduced myself and we talked about the old days. I was really impressed to see how Johnny was handling the lads. He has a no-nonsense approach to these tough young men and I could see he was very much a father figure to many of them.

I felt a little ashamed that we had such a fantastic sports facility in our Canary Wharf offices, where lawyers can play squash, swim and exercise for free, and these poor kids were paying weekly subs (subscriptions) to train in such awful conditions.

I made a pledge that I would try and do something for the club. I'm not sure that these two thought they would ever see me again.

When I got back to work, I mentioned the club's plight to our senior partners and managed to get a £500 donation from our charity group.

Nuffield Proactive Health, who manage our health club, also gave me £150 and diverted to the club four exercise cycles that were due to be scrapped.

The guys were delighted when I turned up with these and the £650 cash for them to buy some new kit and equipment.

I knew this would not last long, though. So I came up with the idea of a boxing dinner show to raise some lasting funds for the club. It turns out the club have never had such a show, where tables of more wealthy boxing fans are entertained to fine dining and wine and a night of boxing. In fact, they had never had their own show, full stop.

So I decided to contact one of our clients, George Iacobescu, the CEO of Canary Wharf Group. I wrote to him, telling about my life in Wapping long before the Canary Wharf development was built, my association with the boxing club and about this book.

I asked him if he would let me have the East Wintergarden at Canary Wharf for free, so that I could hold this huge dinner/boxing show for the club, and his response was immediate. "Yes, of course, I loved your story and can't believe that you lived in this area at a time when all the docks were open."

This hall normally costs users around £8,000 a night and, to add a bit of class to the event, the hall would be dressed fantastically for Christmas.

I then set about inviting all the property and construction contacts I have made over the years, and they all agreed to take tables of 10 at £900 a throw, which covered the £23,000 cost of the catering.

The date was set for 28 November 2008.

News spread fast and I was interviewed on the national radio show TalkSport by the Radio and TV sports presenter, Danny Kelly, who thought my work in bringing this little boxing club to prominence to be worthy of a time slot on his talk show program.

I also traced ten of the guys I used to work with at Trollope and Colls in the 60's and they all came to the event, along with all my old pals from Wapping.

Three of the five Wapping boys that fought on the club's first ever boxing outing in Tilbury in 1965 were present on the night.

The current Professional Super Featherweight World Boxing Council Champion, Nicky Cook, came along too with the UK's version of the USA's "The Contender" boxing show host, Michael Lomax. Jimmy Flint was also there. I called the trainers of the club up into the ring to join me and these celebrities for a well deserved recognition of all their hard work with the club.

303 dinner guests were greeted with glass of champagne on arrival before sitting down to a fine dining experience and close-up card magicians at their tables.

A further 150 local fans paid £10 each to watch the fights from a balcony above the dining hall.

A TV cameraman was on hand to show all the fights on the big screen in the hall and the boxers all received a DVD of the bouts.

The boxers entered the ring to the rousing sound of their favourite tunes, The Eye of the Tiger (The Rocky film theme music) and Simply the Best by Tina Turner, etc.

I held an auction in the ring at the interval, with diners bidding for donated prizes such as nights for two in the top hotels at Canary Wharf, balloon flights, seats at both West Ham and Arsenal corporate boxes, car racing and golfing hotel breaks, a Cessna flight up the Thames, autographed boxing gloves, etc.

Over 450 people attended the show and it raised in excess of £8,500 for the club.

The night was a spectacular success and I was absolutely overwhelmed by the response to the event and the generosity of everyone who came.

The event came at such a fitting time for me, just as I completed this book.

I seem to have come full circle in my life, bringing Wapping to Canary Wharf, if you like.

Who knows, maybe this could have been the event that launched another young East Ender's career. Maybe we found an Olympic Boxing Champion for the London 2012 Olympic Games on this night.

2008
The times they are a-changing

*"Hundreds of staff in the City of London and Canary
Wharf and, indeed, our own offices
are losing their jobs".*

So what is happening to me right now and why did I write these memories down.

Life has changed so much since my time in Wapping from 1952 -1982.

Sadly, I've just had to watch my best friend, Danny Ferry, who had that bleeding awful holiday with me in Benidorm, die of cancer at the ridiculously young age of 55.

Danny's brother rang me at the end of November 2008 to say that Danny had been diagnosed with terminal cancer and, even more shocking, that he had just weeks to live.

Danny had separated from his wife, Teresa, many years ago and never got over the loss of his family unit. He had two (now adult) children, but was living alone in Wapping following the death of his mother, Margie, just a year earlier.

I would make sure I saw Dan at least one Friday in every month.

I was shocked to see how quickly he was deteriorating and alerted all his old Wapping mates. I would visit Dan in the London Hospital every working day until Christmas Eve 2008 to try and keep his spirit up.

He slipped away just after Boxing Day.

From the day I learned of his fate, I vowed to myself and Michael that I would carry his coffin at the funeral. I would enlist four other friends, too. Football skipper Tony "Razzle" Ransome, brothers Terry and David Sapsford and one of Danny's drinking pals, Wayne Massett. Dan's brother, Michael, made up the sixth pall bearer.

One of my team at work enlarged a great photo of Danny in his football kit for me and that was placed in the church.

It rained on the day, but Michael asked that he and I walk behind the hearse carrying Danny as we proudly led the cortege through the streets of the East End where we grew up to St Patrick's church.

As were about to lift the coffin from the hearse, Danny's estranged son arrived, and Wayne stepped out of the line to allow him to join us.

I'd tried hard to get as many people as I could back to Wapping for the mass, and it brought a lump to my throat as we entered a packed church.

Michael led the bidding prayers and, after Mass, I gave a personal eulogy to my friend, ending with the poem "Do not Stand at My Grave and Weep" by Elizabeth Frye.

I held myself together and managed to get through it without bubbling, but I crumbled a little when the church filled with applause as I left the altar.

We later held a shorter service at the City of London Crematorium in Newham, which ended with the song Danny Boy being played as the curtains closed on Danny's life and our lifelong relationship.

The sun suddenly burst through the stained glass windows of the chapel and the music faded.

As we stood outside admiring the flowers, Danny's son thanked me and I pressed the photo of his Dad in his prime into his chest as a keepsake.

We drove back to Wapping and raised a few glasses to our pal.

It was a wonderful and fitting end. A day I will never forget.

I woke the next day feeling that we had done our best for Dan. My friends and his family were very complimentary about the eulogy and having his pals carry him and said I'd brought back a bit of the old East End spirit to Wapping. At least for a day, anyway.

My daughters, Kelly and Louise, are still at home with Maria and me, and life is still good. The girls are grown up now. Kelly is 22 years old and a university graduate; Louise is 17 and studying for her GCSE's, and will almost certainly follow her sister into university. Maria still works for Barclays Bank. As part of her charity work, she also helps out a young Turkish refugee and her child.

I'm still travelling the world, and recently flew to Abu Dhabi and Kiev in 2008 to find, and then help our business fit out offices in regions where we have never operated before.

In the last year, I attended a Peace Conference in our London office at Canary Wharf where Gerry Adams shook hands with Colin Parry, the father of Tim Parry, the young lad blown up by an IRA bomb in Warrington.

As they did so, I glanced from our level 30 function rooms onto the site of South Quays Plaza, currently still under reconstruction after being blown up by the IRA in 1997.

Quite an amazing evening.

Irish terrorism seems to have ended and Catholics and Protestants are sharing power in Northern Ireland. Meanwhile, London is now under threat from Islamic extremists who want to bomb their way of life onto us.

My former employers, Lehman Brothers, who were one of the world's leading Investment Banks, have disappeared entirely in London, and Mike Collier, the guy I put into my role before I left, will soon be out of work.

The banking industry has just collapsed due to the "credit crunch" in the U.S. and this is having a grave effect on business in the UK where we appear to be heading into a possible two year recession.

Hundreds of staff in the City and Canary Wharf and, indeed, in our own offices, are losing their jobs.

Despite this, I played a significant role in letting 90,000 sq ft of office space to KPMG, one of the major accounting firms in the world, and have just agreed to let a further 32,000 sq.ft. to MasterCard.

This particular deal was struck at a time when only 40,000 sqft in total changed hands in the City of London throughout the whole of January 2009.

I was recently invited to speak at a tough school in Thamesmead. I told the assembled schoolchildren that there are still careers out there for them, providing they don't pigeonhole themselves into what they believe life has set out for them.

I told them. "Reach for the stars, don't ever put yourself down. Look for the doors of opportunity and try to open them up, and, who knows what you might achieve. Whenever you get knocked down, take a step back and take time to recover, because you will. Don't tell me that you've had it hard and it's not possible to do well because you come from the wrong side of the tracks. Believe in yourself. Make time for people, work hard and play harder. It has taken me forty years to become an overnight success".

London's East End continues to change. It has always welcomed immigrants, from the Huguenots, the Jewish and the Irish communities. All of whom integrated with the indigenous East Enders

The Wapping area, and Tower Hamlets in general, is now increasingly becoming populated by the poorest of the Bangladeshi community, who occupy the aging council properties

We are also seeing a great influx of the wealthiest of yuppies who now like to have a "pied de terre" warehouse conversion apartment on the river, and the place doesn't seem know itself any more.

Neither of these groups seems wants to integrate, really, with anyone outside of their own lifestyle, and the community spirit I knew seems to be a thing of the past. There's a strange, religious and cultural divide in the communities that inhabit the place now. But I suppose we had that between the Protestants and the Catholics when I was young, anyway.

Most of the people I grew up with and lived alongside have now followed my reluctant lead and moved away to areas such as Becton, to the east of the docks area, and out to Hornchurch, in Essex, and have left the new East Enders to it.

So why did all this happen to me?

"We had nothing, but we had everything. Things that few in East London seem to have today. A wonderful community, a close family life and a strong work ethic"

Here I am in 2009, typing these words into one of the four computers in our house. Sitting comfortably in my office den, I'm listening to some old 50's music on my iPod.

But my mind is drifting back to a time when life was tougher, but somehow better. Not materialistically, of course, but there was really something special about living in Wapping back in the 50's, 60's and the 70's.

We had nothing, but we had everything. Things that few in East London seem to have today; a wonderful community, a close family life and a strong work ethic.

We had fun too

We didn't need mobile phones, BlackBerrys, the Internet, hundreds of TV channels, MP3s, etc, and life was lived under a different code of practice.

If we fell over as kids, our Mums would spit on their handkerchiefs and rub their spittle on our wounds to make them better. The mums of today are more likely to reach for their mobile phones first to text their solicitors and try and sue the arse off someone.

Kids don't play out like we did any more, but sit alone in their bed rooms "communicating" with each other on Facebook or MySpace websites.

My space was the playground in our flats, and my face was filthy most of the time.

We'd put coats down and play 20-a-side football matches with a real ball. We didn't have virtual matches sitting on our sofas in front of the telly with some hand held device as company.

I recently passed a skip in our street. There were two brand new kid's bikes in it. That sums it up really. Kids don't go out to play and parents today are generally so much better off that they can toss those bikes away so easily, and no-one (travellers aside) would want to be seen to take anything from the skip.

In the 50s, I used to make my own bikes from the odds and sods of discarded cycles I'd find on bombsites.

In writing this book, I've bared my soul and told you many things, about my feelings at the time of my parents' deaths, for instance. Those were incredibly painful times for me and my brothers and sisters.

No kid should lose their father at such a tender age, or have to witness his long and painful death, or have to discover their mother dead without any prior warning, like my brother Robert did, or to have to suffer giving her the kiss of life in a fruitless attempt to bring her back to life, like I did.

I've written about my personal pain, but these losses also happened to my brothers, John and Robert, and my sisters, Pat and Catherine. Sharing this pain brought us closer together, where perhaps some families would have torn themselves apart.

In the course of writing my life story, I had to make a decision. Should I tell you everything? Well, I have.....almost.

So what actually made me become the person I am today?

Why was it that I had to be the centre forward in our football team, and at the forefront and not just one of the team?

Why did I need to be the wicketkeeper in the school cricket team and not just a fieldsman?

Why did I become a boxer and have 30 fights and was not just happy to sit at the ringside and watch?

Why did I go alone to the World Cup Final in 1966 when every other 14 year old was happy to watch it on the telly?

Why did I decide to take up an apprenticeship in 1967 to become a skilled electrician instead of taking one of the better paid jobs my friends did at the time, like scaffolding and laying tarmac, etc?

Why was I not content with becoming a qualified electrician in 1972, but felt the need to gain even more technical skills and become an air conditioning engineer?

Why did I need to entertain people in the 1970's as a DJ in the pubs and night clubs in the East End and go on to become, what some would tell me, the most popular wedding DJ in North and South East London ?

What drove me into management roles in1986, when many of the people I worked with were happy to stay as one of the shift workforce?

Why, with my confidence at its lowest in 1990, did I then contact the world's largest law firm and tell them that they needed me to manage the largest single-let building in the City of London?

What drove me to run the marathon in 1989 after injury had forced me to give up playing football in 1979?

What drove me on to run 10 London Marathons for charity when most are happy to stand at the side of the road and watch them?

Why did I become the Chairman of an apprentice training organisation to encourage other young East End men to reach their full potential?

How, with no education to speak of, did I end up travelling the world in business class, advising lawyers in Moscow, Dubai, and Delhi, etc, on how to select and design their new buildings?

How the hell did I, that scruffy little kid from Wapping, end up managing one of the largest and most expensive properties in Canary Wharf?

Why did I feel the need to hold that fantastic boxing dinner show and raise so much money for a boxing club that I have not been to since I was 14?

What is it that is so different about me?

Well, I'm not into psycho-babble, and I haven't spent my life contemplating my navel. Nor did I waste any energy or time looking for someone to blame for my difficult start in life. I just got on with it and made the best of every opportunity that either came my way or I created.

I've always viewed life as a series of "doors of opportunity" beyond which there is always another set of doors. You can either stay safe in each lobby or open (or kick down) the doors in front of you to move forward to the next set of doors. Although I didn't know it at the time, deciding to take up an apprenticeship in 1967 was the key to my very first door of opportunity.

But while I have been sharing my innermost thoughts and memories with you, I have kept one secret from you.

I spoke of how secure we all were in our island community, locked away by road bridges from the rest of the world. Down there in the heart of the London Docks, surrounded by huge dockers who'd tear the head off anyone who would dream of hurting us kids, we felt we were as safe as houses.

Well, but not always.

A stranger came into Wapping one cold winter's night, and he wasn't looking for The Prospect of Whitby pub, either.

He lifted me off the streets and took me away with him, away from all I loved and those who loved me.

My cousin Peter and I were playing outside the Jolly Sailor pub. I was about 8 years old.

A man on a motor scooter stopped to talk to us. He asked us if we wanted a ride on it, which we did.

But we weren't silly and said we could not be parted. He said that was ok and that he would give me a ride on it first and then return for Peter. This made sense to us and I got on.

It was cold and I had to hang on tightly to this man in front of me as we sped through the streets. I was enjoying the speed but getting worried, as I did not recognise where we were anymore.

He pulled onto a bombsite and stopped the scooter to talk. I was shivering by now. I didn't think it was odd being there. It's the type of place we played on as kids all the time.

He saw I was shivering and put his big woolly scarf around my neck, which was warm, and I felt better. Then he pulled me slowly towards him and put his arms around me. I still didn't realise there was anything wrong at this stage, apart from not knowing where I was.

He turned out to be a nonce. Paedophile was not a word in use at the time, of course.

For the life of me, I couldn't understand why he was fumbling around inside the front of my shorts. I knew that it was not right and started to panic a bit and said I wanted to go home.

He took me back to where Peter should have been, but he had gone. The man took the scarf off my neck and drove away. I was one of those lucky kids who came back home from such an experience instead of being murdered.

I have no doubt in my mind now that the scarf he put around my neck would have been used to strangle me, if I had created any fuss.

I ran upstairs to number 218 Riverside Mansions and into my bedroom and burst into tears. Mum wanted to know what was wrong, but I couldn't say anything because I was in shock, and Dad would have given me a good hiding for going off with a stranger despite all the warnings that I'm sure I would have had.

We didn't need or ask for counselling in those days, but I was scared of Dad and decided to stay stum and keep it all to myself.

But putting this down on paper and being able to openly talk about it now has been an enormous emotional release. I should have had that release 49 years ago, and I know now that, of course, I should have told my Mum and Dad.

They went their graves not knowing that they could have lost their son that cold night in Wapping all those years ago. I wonder what would have become of my family if they'd have had to live with that.

I now firmly believe that being lifted from the streets by that stranger and made to stand there shivering on that bomb site in1960 had affected me more than I ever knew.

Some say that you see your life flashing past you at those moments, but I was so young that I had no life experiences to flash past me at that time.

Luckily, I came back from my ordeal where so many other young kids disappeared without a trace, and, in writing this book, I have allowed my life to flash past both my own and your eyes too.

I kept that secret until 2005 when I told my wife Maria about it. She was the first to know. But the hardest thing I've ever had to do was to tell my two adult children, Kelly and Louise, this year of my stupidity all those years ago.

I could barely speak the words aloud. It was as if that scarf was being pulled tightly around my neck as I struggled to get the words past it.

I have had a completely different relationship with them to the one I had with my own father, and I have no doubt at all that they would have confided in me if this had happened to them.

So my dreadful secret has now been released. The genie is out of the bottle and that man can no longer haunt my mind.

I have finally beaten him and he cannot affect me any more. I've won and, unlike him, I can be happy with everything I have achieved and how I have lived my life.

I now believe I had been subconsciously trying to show the world (or maybe just myself) what it would have missed had I lost my life that night all those years ago.

I certainly haven't been able to find any other reason for my overriding need to make so much of every single opportunity that life delivered to me.

So, if you have been keeping a secret within you for years, please take up a pen and start writing ,or sit at your computer and start typing, and release your own personal genie from that particular bottle!

It works, believe me.

Thank you for staying with me on the journey of a lifetime from Wapping to Canary Wharf, and may your God protect you all on your journeys as much as he has protected me on mine.